MANAGEMENT
MANTRAS

One can view management in it's
entirety only after compr
on our planet in its fu
That's how one could
real pleasu

Maturity lies in having knowledge
and its good use in practice in
day to day life.
In order to make meaningful contribution for a
comfortable and totally satisfying
entire humanity's strife.

Col. Ravi Batra

PARTRIDGE
A Penguin Random House Company

ISBN: Hardcover   978-1-4828-1073-8
             Softcover   978-1-4828-1074-5
             Ebook   978-1-4828-1072-1

Address
Colonel Ravi Batra
20, Bercha Road
C/o KLP. Post office
Mhow (M.P.) 453 442
e-mail : batraravik@hotmail.com

Cover Designed by My daughter:
Pooja Batra (illustrious Bollywood Actress.)

To order additional copies of this book, contact
Partridge India
000 800 10062 62
www.partridgepublishing.com/india
orders.india@partridgepublishing.com

Translated Version of
Swami Swarupanand Saraswati Ji Maharaj's
Foreword

I ndian seers and saints had contemplated on life with great
concentration and intellectual maturity. Hindus have managed to
exist as followers of the faith despite a variety of odds, uncongenial and
dangerous times over the annals of our history. Today, our great nation's
heritage is known in the world as a result of time-tested life
philosophies as given in our scriptures.

In our system, organisation of life in various Ashrams; stages ensures
meaningful management of whole life. Life was divided in these stages
in mind the possibilities of man's synergy, capabilities, potentialities
and grasping powers. In Brahmcharya stage, one was equipped with
knowledge, physical and mental processes. One's personality was to be
developed based on the simultaneous development of intellectual and
body powers. Based on this edifice alone, one could possibly, carve out
one's successful life in the days to come. After this, in 'Grahast
Ashram', it was an important and necessary duty to prove one's
competence and skills learnt in the first stage. In order to mull over and
concentrate on the practical knowledge gained during the second stage,
Vanprasth was devised. During this third stage, after gradually
relinquishing the wordly materialistic responsibilities, a formidable
basis was laid to enter the fourth and final stage; Sanyas Ashram. In the
twilight of anyone's life in those days, the life was like a beacon and
worth emulation. It looks as if in this stage, one is without social duties,
obligations and responsibilities. Whereas, it isn't true. In-fact life in the
fourth stage is only dedicated and meant for the general welfare and
well-being of the society. Due to this last phase, Indian society
continued to be enlightened and enriched.

Besides, the organisation of whole life into these phases or stages, our
scriptures kept us aware and warned about man's intellectual
inadequacies, angularities aberrations and immaturity. These gospelled
to remove 'I' and 'Me' in both thought and deed in order to wipe out
pseudo pride as a result of which, man felt truly liberated.

Soul being witness to one's each act, life was moulded within the
bounds of strong character and matured intellectual heritage. With this

concept, man was motivated to lead life of discipline, devotion, duty-consciousness, concentration and sincerity. These tenets are significant and fundamental sources for real success in life.

With the dawn of modern age of new discoveries and inventions, our religious scripture's scientific temper has been more than proven. It is most unfortunate that we Indians today blissfully ignorant of great knowledge as bequeathed to us and take pride in blindly aping the West. Col. Ravi Batra has made a sincere, matured and laudable attempt to highlight through his Management Mantras the great advantages of ancient Indian ethos of Management. He has, in our age, written about life-management which is the most talked about subject of our times and has proven most forcefully and convincingly that our ethos of management of life as enshrined in our scriptures is a unique model and an ideal and most practical art of life-management.

Those, who are inquisitive to know how to succeed in life, will get a very healthy and matured glimpse of the same in this book. They will also be motivated to ponder over age-old intellectual heritage. The unique style of presentation of authors in the book has made it all the more interesting and captivating. Such like books must also be translated in Hindi and other Indian languages.

I congratulate Col Ravi Batra; the author of Management Mantras for such as magnificent work and hope that our young generation will lead meaningfully successful life by following and practising both in letter and spirit the tenets, concepts and vision as enshrined in the book in their day to day life !

Bhopal

Swarupanand Saraswati
(Jagadguru Shankracharya Jyotir Peeth
and Sharda Dwarka Peeth)

Foreword

Management, as practiced and theorised today is made out to be a complex subject, difficult to be comprehended by a common man. The specialisation in the subject has spawned several theoreticians and practitioners whose works are being studied by students of management worldwide, in pursuit of scholastic excellence. Like in any other discipline, new concepts and theories have given rise to a whole lot of expertise leading to systematic study of management as a discipline.

In our search for specialisation and excellence, we, however, tend to forget that much of what we manage is taught to us by life. The experience of living is the greatest of all experiences and life is the greatest of all teachers. The true expert in management is the one who comprehends life in its entirety and draws lesson from it for wholesome life management.

Col. Ravi Batra's 'Management Mantras' looks at life from a different angle but with an expert eye. The contents lean heavily on Indian spirituality and lead us to look at life from a whole new perspective making the comprehension and management of life far more easy and palatable. The contents in the verse form, which are both lucid and rhythmic dwell deep into issues concerning whole life management drawing upon ancient Indian wisdom and ethos. Neatly arranged verses guide us through a journey of life where we learn to use our mind more constructively to realise our maximum potential.

Col. Batra has put in high quality efforts to bring out a work which deserves equally high appreciation. I congratulate him for the stupendous effort and wish him best of luck and success. I am sure, you will enjoy reading the work as much as I did and more importantly, learn your lessons on life management which, will make living a far greater experience.

Bangalore
21st September, 2004

M.S. Kapur
(C.& M.D of Vijaya bank)

Acknowledgements

1. I am grateful beyond words to his holiness; Swami Shankracharya Swarupanand Ji Maharaj for his most gracious, benign and divine encouragement through his foreword to my book. I would remain indebted to him life-long.
2.   I am thankful and grateful to Sh. M.S. Kapur; Chairman and Managing Director of Vijaya Bank for his kind foreword and also to Sh. Shenoy; Chairman & Managing Director Bank of Baroda for patronising my book and helping me to reach out to masses so graciously.
3. I also thank Army Head Quarters, New Delhi for recommending my book for libraries of all Indian Army Units and Institutions.

----

*Dedicated to
my wife; Neelma in whose
loving & caring company,
I've looked at life from a
different view point*

CONTENTS

UNIT - I
UNDERSTANDING LIFE

UNIT - II
ROAD TO SUCCESS AND HAPPINESS

UNIT - III
PRACTICAL LIFE MANAGEMENT

UNIT - IV
MANAGEMENT IN THE CONTEXT OF OUR 'GLOBAL VILLAGE'

UNIT - V
ANCIENT INDIAN ETHOS OF MANAGEMENT AND ITS ALL TIME RELEVANCE

♦

AUTHOR'S FOREWORD.....

One can view management in it's entirety only after
comprehension of life on our planet in its full measure.
That's how one could practice it with real pleasure.

Life in any form is managing it's peculiar environment
ever since it's very inception.
Our cumulative knowledge on the subject however, is,
yet a very small fraction.

Let clear understanding of truths of life and promptings
of our inner conscience guide all our activity.
So that, we could experience blissful peace, joy and happiness
in
life-long festivity.

Hindus since times immemorial, had devised and
practiced perfect management of whole life
and had, along with all-round physical, mental and
spiritual development, made the whole span a peaceful,
serene, calm and pleasurable strife.

Business and professional pursuits in life are an important part.
Therefore, it needs to be attended to with a diligent,
honest and sincere heart.

Through this effort, I've endeavoured to make you
learn to use your mind in a new way
and guide you to use your maximum potential in a positive
manner without losing even one more precious day.

Obviously, I can't quench your thirst for knowledge
but, certainly, can help keep the spark of inquisitiveness
and inquiry aglow.
I can't suggest ready-made solutions to all your problems
but, certainly, can help you have a serene and calm life-flow.

1

UNDERSTANDING LIFE

LIFE

It's an uncontrolled dream
        abruptly ends.
It's a mountain of smoke
        with indistinguishable and unpredictable bends.

You care for your body so much
and to satisfy it, materialistic pleasures you search.
At the fag end, the same leaves you in lurch.

Flesh and bones are only a cage for the soul.
It's upliftment alone, should therefore, be your only goal.

You set your heart on unreal and mortal things
        and wasted a fair chance.
Live with Him every moment in meditation and trance.

How's your life different from that of an ant who
        also, lives full life cycle and dies ?
If you, didn't see Him every where and lived on white lies!

Remember Him, sing His praises and do what He says.
For achievement of 'Moksha' (A state of total freedom for
soul when it doesn't take rebirth) there are no other ways.

Billions of souls in various attires are wandering
        in dark on the face of our earth.
Remember, very few finally get free from the cycle of birth
and rebirth.
Where is the harm in sincerely trying ?
Otherwise, you came crying, cried through life
        and will also, end up crying.

Like morning stars start receding into oblivion,

so does life spark,
It's cage then appears like fungus eaten tree bark.

Issue of life and death is decided by a breath tender.
Remember, death keeps no calendar.

TWO GREAT REALITIES

Birth and death are only two realities
and rest all, a big crap.
Birth is like waking up at dawn
and death, an unending eternal nap.

In between the two realities, lies a complete life story.
Alas ! almost everyone lives amidst
yet, doesn't recognise His benign glory.

All kinds of comforts and pleasures
He gives, straight in one's lap,
makes one wear many a crown and cap.

Although, He is in and around
and His blessings know no bound.

Yet, one never thinks of Him and keeps Him so far away.
That's exactly where the whole problem lay.

Life without Him, is a sheer experience of suffocation and
pain.
One could feel unfathomable pleasure and solace by just
being humane.

You lose nothing by being a gentleman and kind
whereas, you lose every thing when,
a hapless suffers before you and you turn blind.

No one can hold time as it keeps ticking on,
as, no one can hold sand in the palm grip
as, it keeps slipping down.

Making this gap between birth and death
charming and electrifying, is in one's own hand.
Your deeds alone can make your story remarkably grand.

Seek pleasures through hardships of life.
Once it becomes a habit, thereafter, life will no longer be
any strife.

PASSENGER

I entrained for predetermined destination
and entrusted my life in the hands of the driver; unknown.
Never pondered about his skills and competence
or on that account, gave vent to any moan or groan.

I'd a compartment and seat number allotted to me
and therefore, my environment wasn't of my choice.
I'd to accept the same without making any fuss or noise.

I came across people of all sorts;
some close and some far.
To some, even, I talked freely without any bar.

Some, I found friendly and compatible
and from some, I kept distance.
In the company of some, time flew and
I, unknowingly got closer to my destination.
Some, came in enroute and got down.
Some, were there when I boarded and

were destined for a farther town.

Some, were rich, some not so rich and some, poor.
Some, were aimless travellers and some,
on private or official tour.

Some, were healthy and cheerful.
Some, with unhealthy mind and looked fearful.

Passengers of all sorts were going on the same track
and getting closer to their destinations every second.
For some, thoughts occupied them so much
that they reached destinations before they could reckon.

Track for all, was sometimes straight
and sometimes took a curve,
Some, always kept their cool
and some, lost their nerve.
For some, it was a happy journey
and for some, a big bore.
Some, awaited destination with forbearance and patience
and some, awaited impatiently at the door.

It went over nullahs and rivers.
Some, felt pleased and some had quivers.

Sometimes, the scenery around was a feast to eye.
and sometimes, hands spontaneously went up
waving good bye to passers by.

The driver drove sometimes fast and sometimes slow.
Passengers had no say whatsoever,
and could do nothing but bow.

Train while on move, made sounds

sometimes jarring and sometimes fascinating.
Thus, some shrieked and for some, it was rejuvenating.
Aren't all of us passengers in this life train ?
And, would be on board till our respective pre-determined
destinations came !

JUST REMEMBER

All those, who came this way,
have gone back only one way;

Body rests on same throne and with the same thread
just like, a stone or heap of lead.

In this regard, nobody ever had any say
Yet, out of billions there are just a few
who, at that juncture, were really happy and gay.

Alas ! most of us, merrily keep groping in dark
and somehow keep living as if, within the jaws of a deadly
shark.

There is always that righteous and divine ray.
It's high time to take stock of things around
without wasting yet another day ?
Otherwise, remember, unaffordable price
you'll have to pay.

Yes, it is, a fact that, as one is never too late.
All of us possess that innate goodness,
the practice of which, will make us really great.
No one has carried anything from here ever.
Therefore, how about at the very outset,

stop fooling around and being too clever !

Richest of all, generally, have lived spiritually
the most poor's life.
Only, at the end of the road, did they realise
how wasteful had been their life-long strife.

Your riches and fortunes, remember,
never make you really rich.
Pseudo materialistic fascinations and attractions,
drag you more and more in a hellish ditch.

More you get sucked in, more darkness
in seemingly glittering environment around, prevails.
Net result is that, near your end, you feel just like a helpless
sailor in deep stormy sea without his sails.

You'll do a lot of good to self, if you shun egoism
and remain human at all times.
How about using for suffering humanity your dimes ?
Otherwise, remember, you are a criminal in His eyes
and will be punished here and hereafter for all your
known and unknown crimes.

Just remember !

TIMES DO COME WHEN CHIPS ARE DOWN

Time comes in everyone's life when, one hears trumpet's
sound on the other side loud and clear.
When, one experiences in dry eyes, a silent tear.
When, dew drops on lush green grass, sting like thorns.
When one dreams only about being constantly chased by

rhinos with their mighty horns.

When, star studded sky appears like, about to rain down stones.
When, continuously chill and fear enter deep into bones.

When, Monsoon rain looks like a rain of fire from hell,
When, one constantly hears the funeral bell.

When, it becomes more than apparent that only marks and scars of life are to go along.
I assume then, nothing what-so-ever, entertains one not even, the most favourite song.

At such a time, only through inner strength, one can, triumph and rejoice.
provided, one feels the pulse of inner rhythm and hear inner voice.
It's important to be self-sufficient to face both life and death with smiles.
Otherwise, this short span would look like never ending forced march through unknown miles.

HUMAN BODY

Like clear tea needs a strainer and
a horse owner needs a trainer,
Similarly, life needs a container,

This container grows and then somewhat decreases in size,
many truths and lies remain hidden in it's disguise.

Some containers are big and some, small.
Some short and some tall.

Some fair and some black.
Some sealed and some, with a crack.

Some ugly and some attractive to look at.
Some with real good stuff inside and
some, only junk have.

Some by sheer chance and luck,
get placed in show windows under glittering lights,
some remain hidden on a shelf out of everyone's sight.

Some are in a great demand
and on some, on lookers don't even cast a glance.

All containers have their markings and wrappers
like, all babies look alike but,
are generally in different diapers.

All have pre-written manufacturing and expiry date,
when will they reach consumers house, and
when will they be done with, is a matter of sheer fate.

In these containers, life witnesses a constant struggle
between hope and despair.
People without any desire are indeed very rare.

Like customers are attracted by what's inside a container
and not, how it looks like,
similarly, in human containers,
what's inside is worth a glance
and appreciation and not, what's outside.

STARS ARE FOR EVER

Each dawn & dusk is ushered in by morning & evening star,
so is each life spark.
Morning star of life is mother, in whose womb,
life finds an attire.
Evening star is own increment, who, ceremoniously
        brings an end to this life long satire.
There are some dusks & dawns when sky isn't clear.
The usherer too, in life, sometimes, isn't in sight or
        becomes queer.
Sometimes, these stars are unusually bright,
        heralding a promising day & night.
Similarly, usherer of life sometimes, is
        unusually lovable & sweet.
And, helps make life span enjoyable & rather neat.
Life gets ushered in any where in this world in
        the same known way.
Morning & evening stars anywhere in this world, are
        synonymous of each clear day.
Stars don't wither away; in fact, are continuously aglow
        with the same intensity.
So is the soul, which, wanders in various attires
        with the same propensity.
With each dress, soul gets spiritually either upgraded
        or degraded.
Consequently, the halo around her either gets
        brighter or faded.
In this regard, selfless & kind acts for other suffering souls
alone, could help.

Remember, each such act is life's real achievement by itself !

LIFE DRAMA

It's an unending drama;
A perfect synthesis of pathos, melancholy, gregariousness, excitement and trauma.

All play important roles as stage actors.
Scene, role, type of character, timings, stage settings are some of the uncontrolled tangible factors.

Entry on to the stage is almost similar
but, very familiar.

Some, expect new actor's arrival and await impatiently.
Some, as a matter of routine, watch the beginning silently.
While some, greet each other jubilantly.

What a reception; no clappings, and no ovations.
new one is hung upside down.
& then, some professional gives a whack on his bottoms in a strange town.

The first sentence under dazzling artificial lights
is, a protest in the familiar form of loud shriek.
It spontaneously draws smiles on all around
and all heave thankfully a sigh of relief.

Then onwards, under unknown director, on various stage settings, actor plays his destined part,
performs many a character role under various environments of all sort.

The quality of acting and role
influence both spectators and co-actors.
On this enormously big stage, billions of actors perform
well knit & coordinated roles as different characters.

After the performance, all leave the stage
in a well known common style, in this ever running show.
New actors continuously enter and old ones leave,
as if, in a row.

Some, go unnoticed and some, leave permanent and
indelible imprint on many an onlooker.
To some, audience respects with standing ovation
and for the disappearance of some, they thank the director.

Some, through their part, make spectators happy
and some make them cry.
Some, play double roles and some, fraudulently short cuts
try.

Some, with practice, get more matured in the art
and during the drama itself, become celebrities.
While some, with passage of time, invite only pities.

The director maintains somehow, a judicious balance
between comedy and tragedy throughout the play.
I suppose that's how interest of both actors and spectators
in it, stay !

Right kind of role, right timings, right stage setting, right
type of audience and right kind of promptings
from behind the stage, only a few lucky ones, get.

However, the whole drama is speculative and anyone's guess.
Exactly, like the number of fish in a fisherman's net.

STRESS AND STRAIN

All kinds of stress and strain,
sprout and are experienced somewhere in the brain.

It is both physical and mental;
The one out of love episode,
although very painful, yet, is sweet and gentle.

Our, this God-given body is great ;
more you comfort it, more it yearns.
More you grill it, harder it turns.

Even, too much of happiness causes a peculiar fatigue.
A lazy man experiences too much of it as both his body and
mind are in league.

Attachment is the biggest source of pain,
materialistic illusions and delusions are the biggest bane.
Virtually, they make a man unstable and insane.
Each worldly loss is like a blow on knuckles of hand from a
teacher's cane.

Sufferings and mental afflictions are rather acute on those,
who, live a pseudo life and feign.
Can anyone in open, hope to be dry under a spell of
torrential rain ?
People try detachment too late in life and hence all efforts,
go in vain.

Outward involvement and inward detachment is a well recognized viable and practicable way.
One could attend to social duties and obligations and yet, remain always blissfully gay.

Inner happiness, satisfaction and contentment are invaluable.
You could thus make materialistic stress and strain easily bearable.

A BEAUTIFUL BEGINNING OF A TRAGIC END

The old is an infant and infant an old;
One comes out of infernal mother's womb fire.
the other, awaits to kiss the fury of his pyre.

One has just come and the other about to go.
One has a long part in the life drama ahead and the other has almost finished his show.

One cries for, the other remembers and invokes
from heaven his mother.
No wonder, both remain unusually drawn to each other.

Infant is most peaceful on mother's breast.
Old is just fed up with prolonged rest.

Infant cries and laughs in the same breath, so does old;
remembering, his good and bad deeds.
Others have to help both for their basic needs.

Infant knows not, what is in store.
Old knows not, how many vicious cycles of birth more !

Infant chuckles and kicks at her mother's sight.
Old bent with age, and head oscillating,
can't even cry at his plight.

New born speaks language unknown.
Old wants to plead God, but his words
deep behind lips, drone.

Infant is like the Ganges at it's source.
Old, like it is, at the end of it's course.

Child's face radiates innocence.
An old's terse, callous and tense.

Infant invites spontaneous love and affections.
The old remains drawn in his own reflections.

Does infant know that his years will lead him to infancy ?
Old actually welcomes moments, which will
end his derangement and frenzy.

Relatives pick up infants and happily throw them up in air.
whereas, old suspiciously views his relative's care.

Materialistic delusions on infant's ever growing senses
soon start corresponding.
Old's senses to these totally stop responding.

Infant on birth, yells as a protest to dazzling
artificial lights.
Old also, yells at the time of death with fear of
glimpses of weird after flights.

Infant can either get into or get out of cycle of
rebirth and has a fair chance,

Old intricately webbed in cosmic delusions, is amidst
materialistic trance.

Both symbolize life;
One pure and fresh to go through
rigours of life here.
The other, pure and fresh to go through
rigours of life there.

REALITIES OF LIFE

Defences which lack depth, easily crumble,
people who lack depth, always grumble.
Those, who lack character, have personal defences
only skin deep.
Those, who listen to their conscience, rich dividends reap.

Those, who talk aloud, generally lack guts.
Those, who live in palaces, must also know
how to do so in huts.

Those, who wield powers and become proud,
turn deaf towards the message of humility and kindness,
even when, it is clear and loud.
Generally, wander aimlessly like, a dry cloud
and eventually, suffer a great traumatic rout.

I don't know why, after acquiring riches
through dishonest means, man forgets that
he still has two legs !
Since, he misuses and abuses these riches
for self and near 'n' dear ones, that, in the end,
he only begs.

After accumulating riches, do something
that may, make you feel really rich.
Remember, even in a fair game of cricket,
deliveries are penalised which, aren't well on pitch.

At the fag end, those, to whom you gave everything in life,
also, ditch.
You'll be really wise if, in time, you mend and stitch.

AFTER YOU'VE GONE

World would go on the same way.
Just that you won't be there for any more day.
Fact of life is that, none is indispensable.
Infact, you are similar to a commodity
            which is expendable.
In your own house, at best to begin with, there
would be a framed and garlanded photograph.
Soon, it would pick up dust, fungus and draught.
It would then be moved out of it's original
place to some neglected dark and dingy corner,
garland tattered, frame ant-eaten, glass
cracked, snap not worth a mourner.
Some, would remember you on the day
you vanished from where you came.
Remember, your great grand children and perhaps,
grand children won't even know your name.
You're only instrumental in introducing
new actors to this world stage.
They'll have to perform according to
the prewritten script page by page.

Therefore, don't have illusion that without you,
other's life, would stand still.
Hence, don't unnecessarily kill yourself
everyday while going through life's rut and mill.
Try and make your soul's future bright
by being honest, truthful, loyal and acting always right.
Sooner you realize, better it would be.
otherwise, this materialistic life is
a fool's paradise for Thee.

WE GENERALLY

Advise others about side-effects of drinking alcohol while
sipping a glass of neat whisky.
After unpacking biscuits, think about ways and means to
keep them crispy.

Want people around to do what we want them to do.
And upon hollow successes, by hook or crook, carry a
swollen head and feet bigger than our shoe.

Act without due thought.
Hurl curses upon others and keep cribbing for own lot.

Are heard preaching about subjects related to morality
even out of context.
Are only interested to milk a dairy to own advantage on any
and every pretext.

Value only what others possess.
Avoid the company of friends in duress.

Spit venom, speak of sleaze and find faults with anyone
and everyone.

Put the fear of God in our subordinates by wielding stick
and gun.
Apply rules and regulations to others and not to self
and turn a blind eye to anyone crying for help.

Are ready with innumerable excuses to explain reasons of
failure.
Remain busy in doing tricks to impress and allure.

Keep cutting other's roots and grass.
Revolve our lives around only the boss.

For personal motive, don't mind hitting below the belt.
For a glass of water, expect the great ice-caps to melt.

Prefer the option of easier wrong than harder right.
Keep groping in dark even in broad day-light.

Have only our own selfish interests on top priority.
In the pursuit of such motives, care a damn about society.

Believe in the cult of 'taking' rather than 'giving'.
Keep resorting to short cuts to etch out our living.

We do all this so much over the years that, these become
habits and part and parcel of our day to day life.
That's why, we cry and seek forgiveness for our countless
sins at the end of this hard and meaningless strife.

WHAT A DIFFERENCE

When your butterfly's gone,
everything is there except heart is without a beat.
All's intact except, body is without heat.
Eyes no longer react to any light.

Body rests flat on shoulders without any height

Nostrils no longer blow.
Face is without any glow.

Skin is sensitive to neither cold nor hot.
Mind, for a change, is without any thought.

Despite riches and fortunes,
palms are absolutely empty and bare.
Body no longer needs anyone's care.

Lines on right palm, instead of future, point towards the past.
There's no cosmic energy whatsoever, left in the body cast.

Cats, dogs and carnivorous
birds in near vicinity, don't get a scare
Any kind of threatening and dangerous
environment no longer raise a hair.

All rights stand forfeited except, the last right.
Time is turned into just an eternal dark night.

In nut shell, this world is, as long as
your butterfly is there.
Otherwise, the perishable and
mortal is left behind here.

ONE DAY

It would be your last one,
Of course, you won't know that you're
right there at the finish point of your life-run.

That day, you won't be able to wear
your crown.
You would become a subject of the past in
your own town.

You would leave some tell-tale marks and
some memories; both good and bad.
Some would describe you as gentleman
and some as cad.

You would be lucky, if until then, all
your body organs function normally.
Luckier still, if around you, some gather
and give you a send off formally.

Some get to know what is to follow.
Some, by then, with concerted and constant
efforts, upgrade their souls and some, remain
spiritually bankrupt and hollow.

For some, last moments are that of agony and pain.
Some call it a day as absolutely insane.

Yet, for a few, those moments are of joy and ecstasy;
very peaceful and ushering them into divine fantasy.

Remember, that fateful day would dawn
earlier than you anticipate.
Therefore, how about upgrading yourself to
the extent that, instead of crying then, you
could celebrate !

CLOSE TO ONE'S NATURAL END

Top clean and bare.
Chest coated sparsely with grey hair.

Deteriorating sights.
Unusually long nights.

Sagging zeal and zest.
Disappointment in manly test.

Skin ever shrinking.
Bones ever twisting.

Heart rather whimsical.
Brain rather cynical.

Set of removable sparkling teeth.
Brittle gums beneath.

Tongue on it's own.
Most difficult part of journey all alone.

Bone-joints in perpetual pain.
Vanishing thin line between a sane and insane.

Memory on fast decline.
Weird and berserk mind.

Head and arms without support in a strange dance.
Recognition of near and dear ones just by chance.

All eatables taste alike.
That of dumb and deaf's psyche.

Own images and reflections irreconcilable.
Gestures and mannerism no longer appreciable.

Cursory glance of someone now and then to confirm whether one is on or off.
Familiar walls and roof seem to jeer and scoff.

Body ever losing height.
Man forfeiting all his right.

Left with no desire and quest.
Totally disillusioned with word called rest.

Ever losing body weight.
Absolutely strange gait.

Pushed away from the world into that of his own.
Awaiting to go on another journey once again but alas all alone.

Mere thought of above reality would make anyone follow in life, a straight road.
Leading one with pleasure and ease, to well deserved heavenly abode.

Best would be to think, at the start of each day, about all aspects enumerated above.
You will experience an automatic shift in mind's attitude from anger, greed and ego to just pure love.

CHALLENGE OF LIFE

Birth and death are a mere universal routine,
like smoking is accompanied with effects of killer Nicotine.

One follows the other without a miss.
The gap in between the two realities is however, worth a kiss.

Facing challenges of life as they pose, is living a life of purpose and meaning.
Being shy of them, is a negative mental attitude and a sign of weakening.

Since, someone else has given life, therefore, it is He alone, who, has the right to take it away.
It's actually cowardice on the part of any one,
who, prematurely attempts to call it a day.

Life for none here, is a bed of roses,
it's a judicious mix of sweet, sour and bitter medicine doses.

Those, who don't dose up, remain confined to a bed
and, are as good as living dead.

Everyone passes through this way just once.
Yet, people after thousands of years, distinguish between an angel and a demon for instance.

Life story is accumulation of actions performed during each and every breath.
Since, it's primarily each breath alone,
that denotes life and death.
Living for others selflessly, is a real challenge.
Those, who accept it, can only achieve meaningful spiritual growth and excellence.

Actually, one has to be a true friend to all and all things automatically follow.
That is the surest way to ensure that, life doesn't remain wanton and hollow.

BITTER TRUTH

With dead roots, a tree can't survive,
Without breath, there can't be life.

With grey hair, one can't look young,
there can't be peace, without
the use of benign and soft tongue.

With incompatible company, one
                continues to live aloof,
without support pillars, there can't be a roof.

With hearsay in a court of law, you can't prove,
without effort, nothing would move.

With betrayals, life can't be peaceful,
Without truthfulness and sincerity, nothing
                could be meaningful.

With weak and timid mind, body can't have real power,
without God, thorns of life can't be
                crowned with flower.

With lies & deceit in heart, one
                can't have friends,
without faith in Him, one would
                lose balance over life's bends.

With a plain glass, one can't see own images,
without His blessings, one can't
perceive truth behind cosmic mirages.

YOUTH

Youth belongs to mind,
irrespective of number of years, left behind.

As long as, one keeps picking up world's signals in positive
sense, One is young-regardless of age.
Once, antennas are closed down, that's surely the end
of life's page.

Youth is synonym of will to wage struggle in life.
One is old regardless of One's years, if and when,
there are no goals, pursuits and strife.

Healthy heart and mind pump vigour and vitality in body
without which, life's game would look so shoddy !

It's a treat to see men and women in their
eighties displaying free fall from great heights.
Their skins may have had wrinkles but,
their spirits are like ever soaring up colourful kites

When one's interest in life is over,
old age regardless of years
then, predominantly on One's head, hover.

If you want to remain young till your death,
keep your interests alive and
pursue them vigorously till your last breath.

SHUTTLE GAME

Like, a shuttle cock gets knocked by two players
across a net until, it has a weird flight.

So is, in this materialistic world, any man's plight.

He gets shuttled between players of his conscience
on one side and that of ego, hatred, greed, anger and pride
on the other.
Game starts right from the time he relinquishes the
lap of his mother.

He purposely bends rules of the game in favour of
one for selfish materialistic gains and makes him win.
In the process however, he doesn't realise that
he keeps on committing sin after sin.

He demoralises the player of conscience right in the
beginning by having a tacit understanding with materialistic
self disguised as referee and spectators.
Lets other's score go up with those deceitful,
camouflaged and concealed unsporting baiters.

Player of conscience tries his level best despite,
heavy odds.
But, gets frustrated under the spell of his opponent's
deceptive drops and shots.

A time comes when, it's entirely one sided game.
Player of ego, greed, hatred, anger and pride establishes
supremacy, credibility and picks up name and fame.

Nevertheless, game goes on in man's mind
until, player of conscience, in utter disgust, walks
out of the ground.
Demoralised, dejected and frustrated without a crib
or a sound.

By then, like a badly battered shuttle, man's thoughts
display that weird and wicked flight.
Loses that discretion of differentiating between
a wrong and right.

If, he were unbiased and sensible right from the start,
when score board showed 'love each',
surely, spiritual dizzy heights within his
life-time, were well within his reach.!

LIFE IS A BIG WAIT

My journey from womb to tomb,
had been nothing but, a big wait.
At the end of the road, I don't
know if it's worth love or hate.

In mother's womb, I was waiting
impatiently, the day when, I,
would be free to kick around with His grace.
Outside, as an infant, I always
waited to see out of all, only my mother's face.

I waited the day I could, get on my own feet.
As a school urchin, blessed moments,
when my friend, I could meet.

As a senior school boy and collegiate,
I was seen waiting for my date.
As a young ardent lover,
anxiously awaiting for my mate.

Thereafter, sometimes for exam results or appointment

letter or news of promotion.
or outside maternity wards, holding my breath,
waiting to hear our final results after that big commotion.

My desires to possess comfortable
house and possess best of everything
made me work overtime; all in wait.
Awaited children's marriages, their settling
down and arrival of grand children
and great grand children till date.
I didn't know that my time was running out
at such a fast rate.
Coming to think of it, now, all my life
has gone by in it's spate.

Now, I await moments when
I'll call it a day.
Oh, I'm tired and sick of this agonising wait and
yearn to see at it's climax, only your benign divine ray.

WHO AM I ?

Day in and out, I ask self a simple question;
      who am I ?
I have tried my best but till date, haven't found
the right answer, don't know why.

Simple it may seem, but it isn't so.
Unimportant and irrelevant it may appear, but it isn't
      one out of the row.
Because, it's correct answer will then, make you
ask yourself; so, what are you doing and what's your goal?

I presume, one can get to the right answer only after
one has most truthfully and honestly searched one's soul !

Have I come here only to drink, eat and dance ?
or to keep a watch on incorrigible ones with
　　　　　my sword and lance ?
Am I a sex machine always at work ?
Or is it that my sole aim is to keep increasing my girth ?

Have I come here to propagate irreligious things
　　　　　by being only superfluously religious ?
Or is it that I have to pass through this way
　　　　　by being absolutely non-serious ?

Am I here to pollute world's social and
　　　　　moral atmosphere ?
Or am I going to top the list of big frauds,
debauches and hypocrites here ?
Am I going to be an idealist and moralist only in thoughts ?
Or is it that amidst abundance of water
I'm going to create conditions of drought ?

Am I here to collect only gold ?
And in it's pursuit, keep causing aberrations
and deformities to my psyche mould ?

Am I here to be a piece of amusement for
　　　　　all and sundry ?
Or am I going to look neat and clean from outside alone
　　　　　like clothes from a laundry ?

I certainly need better perceptions, knowledge
　　　　　and clear directions.
Only you, oh ! my God, with your remote, could apply

the required corrections !
Who am I ?

AN EASY WAY

Everyone seems to be busy with his life,
fixes goals & hence strife.

Finds time to be at premium & hence runs around.
Everywhere, he is just watch - bound.

All his efforts & results please only his body & mind.
He's completely forgotten about his soul and
left it somewhere far behind.

Heart, soul and mind have to be integrated for overall best
results and also, in order to avoid failures and insults.

Soul's promptings ie inner voice is equally, if not, more
important than all.
Like, in any game of bat in any form, a ball.

Progress on both fronts i.e. materialism & spiritualism
can go on side by side.
Heart & mind then, keep on reinforcing each other
with trust & faith between them, without anything to hide.

Life, will go on without a pause till, the very last.
Irony is, everyone gets surprised as to how all of
it finished off so fast !

HOPE AND DESPAIR

Hope sustains life.
That's why, all over the world, every one is waging struggle

and putting up with strife.

It also, envisages in it's fold, a lot of pain.

In the gap between expectation and actuality,

hinges whether one remains sane or turns insane.

Hope germinates optimism, and in some, faith and confidence.

When these are belied, one gets unusually perturbed and tense.

Hope and despair are two faces of the same coin.

like, need to kill and killing instinct are synonymous of a lion.

Hope is optimism, while despair, a defeatist attitude.

Paradoxically, any human life is punctuated with these two phenomenons regardless of longitude and latitude.

Without hope and expectation, there is no motivation.

State of mind then breeds negative forces, inducing laziness and mental isolation.

Therefore, to reduce tension, one must harbour realistic hope.

Otherwise, stress and strain of life is rather hard to cope.

FEAR AND REMEDY

Like "Static" effects any receiving station's receptions, so does fear, which, effects any mind's perceptions.

Fear is constructive

as well as destructive.

It comes from the head and grips the whole body.

It disturbs heart's rhythm altogether and then, all actions

become rather shoddy.

Consciousness of pain based on own and other's experience, causes anxiety and fear.
When the same get unbridled, it leads to shedding many a tear.

Fear paralyses both nerves and will,
motivation, morale, spirits then mercilessly it would kill.

Exhibition of cautious fear, however, is being wise,
Whereas, unreasoned one, brings along avoidable sufferings in it's guise.

Generally, we suffer from anxiety and worry even before the malady has come.
Shun the very thought that anything could be so fearsome.

Take your heart and mind away from the subject which causes fear.
Think of Him, seek His benign protection and soon His foot steps you'll hear.

Remember, timid and weak-hearted one dies each day a number of time.
Surrender to unmanliness is unbecoming and infact, against self, a crime.

ANGER

In anger, the demon in you, takes over.
Your expressions and actions then, make you like a hot-air blower.

When you lose temper, you lose logic.

When you blow up, you lose your personality's pristine charm and magic.

How illogical is it to think that,
everyone around, should think 'n' act the way you like
Better would be, to keep cool and mend own psyche.

Anger disturbs your inner rhythm and heat.
It upsets and unhinges your brain cells from their natural seat.

Heat generated, disturbs own as well as other's peace.
In exasperation, thinking ability is the first casualty as brain comes under a great siege.

It's fallacy to think that your anger would fetch desired result,
Imagine what'll happen if everyone around, believes in your cult !

Angry expressions make one look like uncivilized and primitive.
In real terms, losing one's shirt is cost prohibitive.

A Manager or a Leader in a fit of anger is most vulnerable.
When things are visibly going wrong, explicit calmness and coolness on their part, denotes inner strength ; plenty and formidable.

Anger can be suppressed by thinking of Him when nerves get a jolt.
Feeling is like that of a professional horse-breeder when he beholds a promising thorough bred colt.

Blowing hot and cold is inconsistency and inadequacy, great.

Keeping cool at all times, brings in happiness and joy in it's spate.

Remember, your anger won't effect this world's life style, except your own life by occasionally stirring up your bile !

FEARS AND WORRIES NEVER HELP

Everyone has fear of unknown.

People express it through their face, expressions and tone.

Unnecessarily, we keep thinking what lies ahead.

Self-created fears, worries, anxieties, and concerns keep one engrossed during the day and even on the night bed.

A heavy dose of it, makes one feel, as if, living dead.

"Do your duty and leave everything to me" perhaps, that's why Hindu's God; Lord Krishna, had said.

Since, results depend on many a intangible and tangible factor,

We have to believe that our lives, right from inception in womb, remain protected by that invisible Protector.

Everyone depends on Him so helplessly, for each breath. If He wishes, one would get out of a situation in which, there's sure death.

Young Indian bride's fears, before her departure to her unknown husband's house, are understandable.

So is true for a fighter pilot, in time's of war, before a scramble.

But, big question is, how do such worries and anxieties help ?

Except, one has to get ready to face forthcoming situations

after tightening one's belt.
Life without worries, fears and anxieties would be so beautiful !
Solace lies in forgetting results and in just being consciously dutiful.

PAINLESS PLEASURES

Worldly delusions make us experience pleasure and pain.
Extreme pressures of either, makes one weird and insane.

Maximum pleasure with minimum pain, in any act or interaction is every one's aim.

Intellect, reason and experience combine in a remarkable mix, in search of the same.

Emotional attachments with both living and non-living materialistic world, result ultimately only in pain
one experiences, as if, a child totally lost in an unknown lane.

In His benign and gracious company, one forgets to feel worldly pleasures and pain.
Remains at all times calm, serene, sublime and genuinely sane.

Pleasure of His kind and benevolent company is pleasure in ultimate
like one perceived collectively by all senses i.e. touch, smell, sight, hearing, intellect and taste.

One derives it by each breath
until one's seemingly physical death.

His real nearness bestows upon choicest pleasures of worlds ; both here and there.
With radiant and smiling face, you could confidently dare.

Since He is within, you could be with Him whenever and wherever you will.
Then on, life would move on excitingly even if, it were dead still.

Bal Gangadhar Tilak is one example whom, this world's pain didn't stifle;
as, even after getting the news of his wife's death amidst his speech, the brightness, brilliance and vigour of his thought didn't, muffle.

All that one has to do is to experiment just once anywhere, any day.
Otherwise, real pleasures, although at your door steps, would remain at bay !

RISE AND FALL

Moon waxes and wanes in the lofty skies,
as if, it, lives and dies.

Ascent and descent are inherent in life,
as if, two faces of the same coin.
like, as distinct and different in looks
are, head and tail of a lion.

All kingdoms in the past reached the climax of their power and then got completely wiped out.
Gain and loss are enshrined in every facet of life, no doubt.

Everyone grows to zenith of physical beauty and power

and then, degradation and degeneration in body cells commences, heralding the final hour.

Therefore, there is no wisdom in vanity
as, affording everyone various climaxes in life, is just His divine amenity.

It is good to think big, but better to stay on mother earth. Similarly, before buying a plot to settle down, it's wise to ponder, about environment of your proposed hearth,

Each wave has it's ups and down.
Even the most sober variety of canine when
driven against wall, can turn into a ferocious hound.

Life is complex yet, not all that hard to understand.
Those, who think rationally and dispassionately,
can definitely turn their stories unusually grand !

ESSENCE OF LIFE

Whether you are burnt or buried how does it matter !
Your dust, in any case, is going to mingle and scatter.

What you do while you live, is significant and sacrosanct and that is the only fact of the matter.
Also, upon had your life upwardly moved towards super consciousness or remained static like an unaddressed letter !

Also, has your body, heart and mind produced rhythmic symphony or continue to rattle !
In other words, evaluate yourself by asking self ; did my soul during life time improve upon it's quality and upgrade itself and felt better ?

Everyone, who comes here, lives a life some how.

What good is it, if, you remained throughout,
egoistic and proud and at the end, for forgiveness, you
bow!
Life is a sum total of actions
inter-se-relations and interactions.

If at the end, for you, none has any time
since, everyone around is instinctively or impulsively busy
collecting his dime.
Don't feel bad and hurt
because, this materialistic world is cunning and curt.

Your world rather than external is internal and you alone
are the master of this vast and endless empire,
the brightness and darkness, gain and loss, success and
failure of which, is, only a matter of perceptions oh ! my
sire!

If you train your vision, it is bigger than countless universe.
If you don't, it is worth condemnation and many a curse.

Your birth and death are two revolutionary stages of your
soul.
Former ushers you into materialistic heaven or hell and
through the latter, you either pitifully wander in abject
ignorance in other forms of life or into an eternal immortal
spiritual slot, you dive roll !

BEGINNING AND END ENSHRINED IN ONE

All of us have to, one day, go to His abode from where we
came.
It's a story of 'one-n-all' and age old same.

Soul changes only her mould
and cast it off once, in her perceptions, it's cold.

Transformation into various forms is every soul's on going struggle for her search of spiritual emancipation.
Until then, she keeps wandering without any inhibition and hesitation.

Each one has to suffer the usual run of the grind.
Without it, final destination no one would ever find.

Performance of selfless deeds in human form for 'one-n-all' can only get there soon enough.
Otherwise, your butterfly would keep hovering and flapping wings ending in a big huff.

Wisdom lies in grabbing this opportunity and going for it. Remember in the game of Hockey, goal get's scored if in right direction at the opportune moment, you push, scoop or hit.

It's an experiment worth a genuine try.
Otherwise, be prepared to end up in sobs and deep sigh !!

Our souls are intense cores of all the cosmic energy.
Our actions backed by our souls undoubtedly, produce unimaginable synergy ;
most essential for any meaningful success.
Otherwise, our actions without backing of inner conscience, would cause only mental agony and limitless duress.

TRUTHFUL ANALYSIS OF LIFE

Living life is life.
Life is, bracing life's strife.

It offers opportunities and threat,
elation and cold sweat,

A mixture of moments both happy and sad,
behavioural stints of a gentleman and cad.

From whatever one does, one derives either satisfaction or
dissatisfaction
which, can't be quantified or measured in fraction.

From cradle to coffin, everyone's story is same.
Difference however, is only in it's title or name.
Whether it culminates into happy or sad end, is most
uncertain.
Also, unpredictable is the time to close and draw out life
curtain.

Life has many low and high tides, which need matching ups
and downs of a stable mind,
otherwise, life could be a veritable mess and cause a hard
grind.

Don't let the world influence your positive nature
and try to build in your own eyes a high and big self-stature.
Don't get ruffled at what would any one say !
Keep deliberately the anti-conscience thought at bay.
Life dances on the beats of joy and sorrow.
Wisdom lies in getting engrossed with today and forgetting
about tomorrow.

Because, who knows will there be any tomorrow or not !
and, what will it unfold as your lot !

Remember, whatever happens, happens for the good.

Have faith and trust in Him at all times, which you should.

Tangible, intangible and unknown factors will keep guiding events in your life in predetermined way.
Over most of these factors you've no meaningful control or 'any say'.

Therefore, relax and let Him do what He has desired for thee.
When in doubt, seek and search Him out from where ever He be.

You will invariably find the designer of your life in and around ;
in open skies, beneath waters, over and under the ground!!

THAT'S LIFE

Fun of life lies in it's uncertainty and it's unpredictability heightens excitement.
Somehow, by His providence, a judicious balance keeps on providing everyone the requisite enticement.

Gap between achievement and expectation determines moods and sets of mind.
Moments turn into memories which, keep piling and then as our past, are left behind.
Happiness and satisfaction is induced when the tilt on a graph is on positive side.
Then, one feels as if, on a roller-coaster ride.

The curve tilt on minus causes unhappiness and dissatisfaction
which, if uncontrolled, leads one to despondency and utter

frustration.

Amidst happiness, one wishes life million year long
while in gloom, one sees everything everywhere wrong.

Things for all would be both wrong and right
and make them feel to have sometimes heavy head or light,

When chips are down, wisdom lies, in mulling over a decision, because in a haste you'd frighten the best one away.
Think about it with a stable frame of mind, on a cool and easy-going day.

Remember, you aren't the only one going through this kind, of rut.
There isn't a man who, while shaving his beard,
in life, hasn't ever got a scratch or a cut.

Passing through life the way it is, is inevitable and therefore, we might as well enjoy.
Wise is he, who has sharpened his visions and perceptions to see though many a worldly decoy !

❑

2

ROAD TO SUCCESS AND HAPPINESS

IT'S SO SIMPLE

Worldly temptations undoubtedly allure and tempt
Getting out of the influence of temptation requires a herculean attempt.

Therefore, knowingly, it's not worth walking into a place of temptation
and worth insulating one's head against its magnetic field without any hesitation.

For peace of mind, stop doing all that you know you shouldn't do.
and start doing exactly what your inner self prompts you to do.

With multiplication of one's wants, one feels like a beggar.
Without spiritual growth, worldly riches and wealth are like over one's head a dangling sharp dagger.

Remove hypocrisy from life for inner peace and solace
Based on only good and noble thoughts and righteous deeds you would win this life-race.

Become a straw in the cosmic wind and allow yourself to be tossed by God's will.
Without any exception, inception of a bad thought, most savagely, one should kill.

Someone who disturbs other's peace, has no right to have his own.
Ask your enemies, like anger, ego, pride, greed and lust to just leave you alone.

Have trust and unshakable faith in both self and in

your God.
Credit all your fortunes and strokes of good luck in life to your Almighty Lord.

Draw comparisons with 'underdogs' and 'Have Nots' on the material plane
and also, with real saints and seers for spiritual yearning, ascendancy and gain.

For the generation of unalloyed love, look at anyone and everyone as your own manifestation.
With a cosmic and spiritual bind, consider yourself as an important and integral part of one God and His own creation.

Put in genuine, selfless efforts to enrich, charm, strengthen His artistic pieces of work and glory
Then alone, you could leave for others behind worth emulating and a memorable story !

MORALITY

Try and live with your head high,
if you, want to avoid a lot of uncalled for pain and sigh.

I've seen many dying, many times before they actually die.
Believe you me, at that time then, there
is no one wishing you respectfully a good bye.

You can keep the head high only, if you keep your self-respect intact.
It calls for putting your moral values into whatever, one does in effect.

Hypocrisy degrades one's character.
Remember, nothing remains hidden from our eternal benefactor.

We could tell a million lies to others but not one to self.
With what face do we then, seek at the fag end, His blessings and help ?

Some say morally speaking, what's
right and wrong must change with times.
Like, fluctuating is, purchasing power of your dimes.

All that is fine,
but, I ask you one question; Have you seen a lemon orchard owner selling anything else except lime ?

Truthfulness, steadfastness and self esteem could only help you keep head high with honour and dignity.
Otherwise, you could keep groping in dark till eternity.

Therefore, deal with the world with your chaste innate goodness and benevolence,
and charm this world with your pristine simplicity and childhood innocence.

WONDERFUL WINDOWS

I see this world through my eyes,
perceive all truths and lies.

I opened them as I slipped out of mother's womb.
Would need someone's help to shut them on the day of doom.

My eyes are inquisitive to see and learn more and more.

Even in deep slumber, I keep sketching behind closed door.
These are most magnificent windows of mind.
Their preciousness can only be evaluated by a blind.

Sometimes, I see things unbelievable,
sharpness of images on mind, absolutely incredible.

They help me formulate my life philosophy.
Coupled with inner wisdom, coax me proclaim sometimes,
a prophecy.

Blessed are those who, through these, form only good and
positive images.
Upon how charming are the eyes on a face, one's overall
beauty and personality hinges.

Through these, I express both love and anger.
Differentiate clearly feminine from a gander.

A good listener conveys his feelings of compassion.
As an intense lover with his eyes, those of passion.

Bright and sparkling eyes denote sun-shine.
Truthful and loyal ones are unusually sublime.

True patriot's eyes have a distinct glow.
A terrorist cast through these on any onlooker, a murderous
blow.

Eyes speak volumes of one's character,
and guide us like, any play by it's director.

If you make your eyes good, you'll see only goodness.
If you let them go berserk, you'll experience only tremors of
brute rudeness.
Eyes also, express shock and grief sometimes, with and

sometimes, without tears.
Through them, unsaid messages are picked up by saints and seers.

How about using them for seeing only goodness and consequently doing good ?
I'm sure, at least, that much, all of us could !

LITTLE THINGS GENERALLY GO UNNOTICED

I derive pleasure in watching ;

Penguine's walk,
cat's stalk.

Flight of a Dragon-fly.
looks of a sly.

Gait of a silk-worm,
Race motor-cyclist over a turn.

Fish jumping out of water,
anyone in a fit of laughter.

Leopard's chase,
monkey in rage.

Tigress cuddling her cubs,
people's moods in city pubs.

A beehive grow,
jet shining blackness of a crow.

A spider netting web,
a toddler's first step.

Looks of a pet dog when in company of his master,

A race horse at a crucial time of race, getting faster.

Parrots and Mainas repeat their name,
match winning goal in a world class soccer game.

Leaps of a deer,
looks of a child who knows no fear.

A weaver bird weaving nest,
a school boy preparing for annual test.

A monkey, on orders, showing tricks.
An ass in joyful mood, exhibiting kicks.

In His beautiful creation, this benign nature and other forms
of life are to be nurtured and enjoyed.
And certainly not meant to be destroyed.

Managers must take out time to enjoy Nature's bewitching
sights.
It would cool nerves, rejuvenate inner spirit and help
achieve better heights.

Mother Nature's signals of perseverance, patience,
genuine care, love, compassion, discipline and innovations
are more than loud and clear.
Application of these tenets in Human Resource
management and development are a must for anyone in
manager's or leader's chair.

HEAPS OF TREASURES

Treasures of joy lie in exploring the unknown.
Expanding horizons of what's known,

Harvesting fruits of toil,
remaining loyal to mother soil,

Avoiding sin,
Considering everyone as just Him,
Being gracious and kind,
having a cool and balanced mind,

Containing pride,
riding a high tide.

Understanding His might,
respecting other's right.

Expressing gratitude,
keeping His company in apparent solitude.

Winning bread through sweat of brow,
putting up an honest and genuine show.

Beseeching blessings from parents, elders and teachers,
and in accompanying truth seekers.

Converting anger into affections.
distributing the same into all sections.

Feeding "Have Nots",
fashioning the gracious life with infinite dots.

Respecting mother Nature's grace.
Sieving reality and truth out of this mad race.

Rendering a helping hand,
sacrificing life for mother-land.

Protecting a weak,
shunning company of a liar and a sneak,

Expressing kind and gracious words,
Loving whole of His creation i.e. even plants, animals,
Insects and birds.

THIRD EYE

All are blessed with divine third eye.
That's how, there dwells in everyone that innate power to sieve truth and a lie.

It is unique as it's invisible and seated deep beneath forehead.
closes, for all times, once, one's conscience is dead.

When it's fully open, it's maverick versatility and fidelity knows no bounds.
Astonishingly, besides, viewing, it can perceive faintest of sounds.

Some listen to their inner rhythms and make it's substantial use.
Thus, avoid falling prey to any cosmic ruse.

It sees objects beyond physical view.
Images are deep, sharp and crystal clear like, on green grass, morning dew.

It is a port from where conscience emits lights of invisible frequency bands.
It's so powerful that, it can beam on anything beyond known distances and lands.

Through it, innate goodness finds mute yet, very powerful expressions.
It can ward off in twinkling of an eye, all kinds of catastrophes and mental depressions.

Without investigation, it can differentiate between fact and fiction.

Impressions gathered through it, are absolute pure logic and get expressed in wonderful diction.

He has, through it, bestowed on all His own sights.
So that, man could understand, the interaction of both visible and invisible worldly lights.

Those, who constantly practice using it for other's good,
develop, in due course, latent powers to hold any serpent by the hood.

Intuition, gut feeling, hunch are all its derivatives.
With quiet consistent practice, one comprehends much without superlatives.

Since most people kill their conscience number of times each day,
third eye remains closed and that Divine telepathic ray doesn't find it's way.

How about making right and apt use of His superb gift ?
Your soul would automatically be upgraded and get that requisite lift.

As manager and leader, one is required to use substantially third eye in order to fathom depth, magnitude and details, with a view to maintain life-train's requisite balance, speed and direction over the rails.

WATCH YOUR MOODS

Your mood,
has something to do with your food.

Weather has a lot of say

and how's been the going over the day.

On the people you came across
and on the mood of your boss.

Thoughts that rake your idle mind,
upon interactions with people; both kind and unkind.

On what your body is used to and what it got.
On yours and your near and dear one's lot.

Upon clothes that you wear,
kind of suffering and privations over the day that, you had
to bear.

Remember, on your mood depends that of many other's,
who have put in a lot at your stake.

Therefore, you have to somehow, manage to have cheerful
disposition even when, you brave tough time or are in dire
strait.

With your deliberate efforts in this regard, life would appear
a cake-walk.

How much have you lived through cheerful moods is, in
essence, your life's quality hall-mark.

Positive attitude would equip one with positive and cheerful
mood at all time.

Remember, Sun, Moon and Stars above us all, don't get
into moods, instead, constantly shine !

CLEAN YOURSELF BY EACH BREATH

Time, place & person has a great interrelation;
wherever, all three get together, person
leaves for his next destination.

All three are fixed & pre-ordained.
There is nothing what-so-ever with the help of which the
same could be pre or postponed

Wash yourself from inside with the soap of recitation of
His name with each breath,
throughout life's length & breadth.

Use perfumes of actions that He dictates
Then, the musk & fragrance around you
would leave mesmerised even those
            who instinctively only hate.

With that, your face would glow &
            radiate like the great sun.
Then, on whomsoever you cast a glance, the
demon in him would get tamed without a gun.

Wherever you look at,
you'll spell innate peace; sublime
and help destroy the demon in others
            who's ever ready to commit a heinous crime
Life is really a very short spell
Its here you decide for yourself
            the place in heaven or hell.

Clean yourself from inside as
early a stage as you can
& then be worthy of being addressed
by Him as His own man.

In communion with God, recitation
of His name would produce such beautiful sound
which, would cause real peace in & around.

People give bath to your body after your butterfly is gone
whereas, life-long from inside you remained dirty
and stinking like a deceitful monk.

You could easily do it if, you have the will.
That's the way the demon & satanic spirits within,
you could kill.

THIN DIVIDING LINE

Really, thin is the line between sanity & insanity.
Collective sanity brings happiness
& prosperity, whereas, insanity,
            enormous sufferings to all humanity.

Naughty demon in us, induces
everyone to do something against established norms.
Cunningly curtains at that time,
            all anticipated nerve wrecking jolts and storms.

Man at that point of time, forgets to hear the inner voice.
Obviously then, what is convenient and
self pleasing, is his choice.

To his horror, he realises soon,
            that, nothing remains hidden.
He then, remains worried and consumed
by the guilt of doing something which was forbidden.

So much so, that, he doesn't get sleep,
then all monsters, snakes, scorpions and
great spiders, in slumber, along with him creep.
Remains restless and loses weight due to fear
            of what may follow.

Thus, age goes by and man remains coward, shallow and
hollow.
Therefore, remedy lies in nipping the evil in It's bud.
Wisdom lies in finding a way which avoids mud.

Hence, one has to listen to inner prompting when
cunning mind is about to dominate.
And thus, help make a promising future
        and better fate.

A COMMON GOAL

I watched pilgrims reaching a shrine
from many a direction.
I saw many a river near sea in a great interaction.
In both cases, goal is one but, more than one ways
like, Sun is one but, innumerable rays.

Similarly, Union with God and with all things
In Him, is the goal of all mankind.
In order to realise Him, we leave many foot prints
on different paths and ways behind.

Life has no meaning other than conscience
realisation of our oneness with God.
Our relationship is analogous to a piece of cloth
with a colour symbol and a rod.

At the end of the road, what good is it
if you are spiritually a bankrupt ?
When you know well that all throughout, ways
to amass wealth had been more than corrupt !

Remember, your birth-right is immortality.

For that, live with Him and shun all kinds of duality.

Love, no doubt is panacea of all ills.
Egoism, hatred, greed and pride, most savagely, it kills.

Therefore, why not just love everyone around
& realise Him before claiming six feet of ground ?

SPIRITUAL PROGRESS

This life is too short to
understand Him & His creation.
Spiritual progress from very early age alone,
can lead one to some sort of emancipation.

Most of us think of Him
only, when we're near our end.
Therefore, we're neither this side nor
the other side of that road bend.

When no one has time for one,
then alone, one tries to speak to Him,
not realising that for such a late start,
        prospects of winning spiritual race are rather dim.

Progressively if one, devotes some time with Him from
an early age, one can make meaningful spiritual headway.
Otherwise, it is futile dreaming about seeing
at the fag end, that divine ray.

Degree of spiritual success depends, no doubt,
 on the earnest efforts made,
like, a hired labourer at the end
of the day, surely gets paid.

It's a fallacy to think that, materialistic & spiritual
progress can't go on side by side.
Remember, both pleasure & body exercise are
inherent in a horse-ride.

For understanding Him,
each breath is important.
For a direct dialogue, one
has to suffer body pain & torment.

Life in human form without understanding Him,
is a sheer waste.
One has to be prepared to suffer all kinds of
privations in order to get that Divine taste.

ALL ROUND ADVANCEMENT

I've watched, women fetching
water in pitchers from a common
village well, many times.
With a row of pitchers on their
head, they walk back
dancing and singing rhymes.
They tread along tracks,
slush and by-lanes,
sometimes, in sun and sometimes
        in rain.

Nothing happens to the row of
pitchers, neatly placed one on top
of the other, which are filled,
        right up to their brim.

These women are of all ages and
    both fat and trim.

Most fascinating part is; not a
drop of water trickles down.
Right up to their houses, they're
absolutely dry including their hair
    and gown.

I reckon that no matter what
they are 'talking n doing', their
mind is tuned to maintain
pitcher's stability.
Past experience of their subconscious
concentration, have given them now
    this ability.

They can go on like this
    any distance,
despite way side attractions and
    resistance.

I think that's exactly how
one should live this life.
Keep tuned to Him at all times from within and
put in all efforts to cope up with this worldly strife.

So that, we don't break pitchers
and get home absolutely wet.
Amidst materialism and worldly
chores, forgetting His blessings,
mercies and our debt.

This is, to my mind, very much practicable.
Perhaps, that's how, we could advance both materially and
spiritually while keeping all along our minds most stable.

BALANCE SHEET

One day, you're bound to get His invitation.
Thereafter, there is no room for your excuse or protestation.
That will be His first and last one.
You'll of course, receive it all of a sudden.
You shall have to go there.
Leaving behind, all that is here.
You can't carry any gifts to please and placate.
In His presence, an accurate account of your deeds
will be read out as on that date.

Your enclosure in that gathering, will be
according to your classification.
His decision in this regard, is final
over which, their is no court with jurisdiction.

You alone, could ensure that, you carry balance
in your account sheet not in red.
For that, only selfless service of suffering humanity
is the best bet.

Therefore, how about changing without wasting
any more time, your very outlook and mentality !
He'll then receive you Himself and extend graciously
all His divine hospitality !

BEST INSURANCE

Niggling doubts of days ahead.
generally cause a heavy head.
What good is in sighing unless the account balance is in red !
Your hopes & fears are your own brain-child.
Given too much vent, mind goes berserk and wild.
To redeem any suffering and torture, have insurance with God.

Pay up the premium regularly from the real wealth stored up in your heart & mind in the name of your Lord.

To begin with, remember Him off & on
and experience your self-created fears gone.

Then onwards, invest in His name every breath
Until, your seemingly physical death.

His insurance would cover not only body but,
your soul.
Payment of premiums won't make you experience
a big drain or a heavy toll.

Also, your soul would remain under insurance
cover till eternity.
As hereafter, you would have become part &
parcel of His own fraternity.

Be wise and invest without wasting any more time.
Otherwise, be prepared to suffer unknown privations
just for a rhyme !

SELF APPRAISAL

I'm on my way out.
I sense fast approaching end of this bout.

With every successive moment, tea in my life's cup seems to be getting cold.
Amply I realize now, that I'm getting old.

I think it's high time, I take stock of things around now.
But, I'm intricately webbed that, I don't know which end to start from and how ?

Over the years, I got inextricably involved with trifles.
In fact, so busy I remained that, I simply failed to notice the speed of passing currents and ripples.

I, myself created those waves and the ripples around me and disturbed my inner calm.
Never pondered about their effect and impact and consequently caused spiritual harm.

Surely, at this stage, I can't undo what I've done except, mend my ways.
Sweep that filth within under the brilliance of Divine rays.

At this rate, I'm bound to get out of the ring in a shameful manner.
After all, what standard of leather can one expect from an amateur tanner ?

I would soon fade out from other's memory and get lost in oblivion of dead past.
I must know, that I occupy some slot in other's brain, only as long as breath in me last.

I haven't lost every thing, as sometime is still there.
All I need to do is, to totally shake up my psyche and for real better days, at least, once dare.

Life in my present form is more than precious.
Without spiritual growth, all other progress is simply a farce and malicious.

Now I do realize, I should have carried out this exercise a number of times as I went along.
Had I done it, I'm sure my whole life would have been a most scintillating and melodious song.

Remember, a pilot keeps on making corrections all along the flight.
That's how, at the destination, he emerges from the cockpit bearing facial looks; most radiant and bright.

HURRY BRINGS WORRY

If you cut out from your life unnecessary hurry,
you would be able to ward off a lot of worry.

You get up late, laze around and then in a bid to be in time,
try and catch a running train or a bus,
invariably get stuck in rush and slush.

Hurriedly you go through the question in exam and start answering without due thought.
After writing many pages, generally realize you fault.

To be in time for a important meeting, you speed up car, generally buy trouble and while on road, own and other's happiness you mar.

In a hurry, you forget to carry office keys and mobile,
and whole day, keep stirring up your bile.

Realize that you are without abdomen guard, only, when, you reach the batting crease.
And, hand over your property on rent without a documented legal lease.

Run across road without a careful glance
and reach some how, on the other side by sheer luck and an odd chance.

This avoidable hurry, cuts short you life span.
Keep cool and live life of discipline and temperance, if you can.

When moments force tension on you, It's certainly the time to stay cool,
like still waters in a deep pool.

Remember, one who's always in a great hurry, is termed a big fool.
Whereas, a calm, cool and meticulous fellow enjoys a long care-free life, as a thumb rule.

LET PEOPLE SAY

Elephant walks by, most unconcerned, when dogs bark.
Soldiers keep penetrating into enemy lines even when it's pitch dark.

Sun doesn't get perturbed when clouds stop it's ray.
We, too shouldn't get unduly bothered about what people would say.

Since, most people around us, have nothing much to do except talk.
If they could help it, they would ensure that you don't even step out for a walk.

However, in any society, if you don't make an unnecessary show of your wife, riches and prayers.
It could save you from a lot of tears.

Every one has the basic right to live the way one likes to, of course, within civilised bounds.
Certainly, our lives can't be dictated and infringed upon by street dogs and hounds.

It never occurs to us that just because there is a street dog outside, we, shouldn't go out of the house,
and not get friendly to someone, for the fear of getting in our hair, a louse.

Remember, whatever is fated, it can't be wiped out.
Whatever one is destined to get in life, one would get it, without a doubt.

POWER OF SILENCE

Silence is rest for spirit and mind
it leaves balance, evenness and tranquillity behind.

It helps in storing up the life force,
unfolds spiritual vision and deeper understanding
as a matter of normal course.

Loud voices of the world drone that of our heart.
Silence; the great unseen power, influences our characters

with a strange contrast.

It works like refreshing rain drops on a hot summer day.
It helps in keeping ennui and passivity in life at bay.

It assists in discovering inherent rhythm, reserves and originality.
Sharpens inner vision, wit, logic and rationality.

In the hour of coordinated silence, realisation of us being His own spark, is more than clear.
It's then alone, this life struggle, we could fruitfully, bear.

It makes us see the finite merging with the infinite,
makes us inwardly wise to discern what's wrong and what's right.
The language of the "Realised " is silence,
That's why in their thought and deed, there is no speck of violence.

Silence means without speech, motion and Worldly agitations and gyration.
It means installing vital energies and acquiring quiescence, serenity and mental stabilisation.

The act and practice of silence changes our perceptions and attitudes for the better.
Harmonises the inner pristine rhythm with worldly notes; the heart of worldly matter.

In higher form of silence, faculties of mind are wide awake and in full light.
That's how, they annihilate the negativity of mind by a massive internal fight.

Fools certainly need to experience it more than the wise. Undoubtedly, it invites inner happiness, pleasures and joys in its disguise.

LAUGHTER: THE BEST MEDICINE

What good is your life,
if, you didn't laugh a while ?

Laughter is the panacea of all ills
Body gets motivated to leave all kinds of chills.

Laughter begets laughter,
with it, this otherwise tardy life, gets softer.

He is admirable, who could laugh under duress.
It's an application of vanishing cream on skin under the influence of weather stress.

One who laughs, has company,
his heart and mind are in good symphony.

Laughter dispels fears of unknown.
Man with good sense of humour is never alone.

Humour cultivates wit and more humour.
Both don't let one fall a prey to any rumour.

Laughing at others is being foolish.
Laughing at someone when he is in trouble, is being mulish.

When one laughs, blood gushes and sunken spirits rise, remember cricket score keeps going up even with leg-byes.

Laughter in life means health.
which is, undoubtedly the most precious wealth.

One who laughs and makes others laugh is the most sought by all.
Humorous man will have for sure, the whole town with his pall.

Witty sense of humour adds to one's charm.
Remember, Charlie Chaplin humoured the world by an invisible storm.

Humorous men live long,
their memories are always fresh and strong.

Charlie is, today, known to people more than Churchill.
All sorts of germs plagueing the peace of our world, for sure, this pill of laughter could kill.

It's recognized and appreciated by all, regardless of caste and creed.
It's undoubtedly the best medicine indeed.

It's spice to life.
like, honey in a hive.

Truth is that, most destitute person in the world is the one without a smile.
Anyone, who hasn't laughed in life, hasn't even lived for a while.

Life is, as it is, tiresome and therefore, let us sing and laugh it away.
This attitude will turn every moment in our life pretty gay.

WATCH YOUR SHADOWS

I notice when I get away from
source of light, only my false
shadows keep growing in size.
That's why, perhaps, I shut my eyes
during the darkness of night & keep
awaiting benign sun - rise.
When I'm exactly beneath that source,
my pseudo shadows just disappear.
Nothing then, distracts my individuality
or true-self from far & near.

This source is light of wisdom that
is inherent.
When it's right on top and takes over,
my whole body is synchronous and
coherent.

When I sway away from that light
of wisdom,
I, only project, pseudo and incorrect
boundaries of my kingdom.

Materialistic delusions alone, pull
us into that area of darkness.
When we get disenchanted with
our false images, we get to that
source of light with unusual fastness.

To keep that light on and stay with
it, is vital.

Otherwise, our stories would
remain without any worthwhile title.

TRUTHFUL RIPPLES

How lonely I'm amongst billions around ?
It's an absolute truth, though, absurd it may sound.
My superficial relations are based on the principle of 'give
and take.'
Pseudo-cosmic delusions put the credibility of my
conscience at stake.

Life goes on as no one is indispensable.
Best time of my life, of course, I was unaware then, was,
when I kicked around in the cradle.

I've yet to realise His company although
He is within me.
I've yet to thank Him for his countless blessings, that be.

Clock ticks away time which, for anyone,
is predestined and unalterable.
I must show superficial involvement with
worldly chores and squabble.

For stability and peace of mind, there is no need to wander
and unnecessarily sweat.
I've to bridle my demands
and think of repaying His debt.

Otherwise, what good are my eyes ?
the value of which, only blind can recognise !

What good are my ears ?

Whereas ton load of silence constantly a deaf bears !

What good are my fingers and nails,
worth of which, only lepers appreciate.
What good are my riches,
if the very sight of a poor, I continue to hate !

Everyone keeps cribbing about shoes
till one comes across a lame.
You've got to be grateful to Him as He gave you
this beautiful form and parents who gave you a name.

When will You help me remove my ignorance ?
When will I help You spread Your universal message of love
and benevolence ?

TRY IT

Little acts of goodness and appropriate smiles,
will endow you with that divine radiance
and keep all evils away miles.

Life gets punctuated with meaningless routine.
Time flies away like a dream.

We don't care if our actions, san humaneness,
politeness and humility.
Thus, we, day in and out, perpetuate the spirit
of devility.

Divine wisdom rests in us
so, let us not subdue.
For all mental afflictions, requisite patience
has the clue.

Time gone by is the past.
There's no good realising it's value when one nears one's
last.

Remind yourself time and again, what you came for
and what are you doing.
Otherwise, there is no end to your wailing and woeing.

Human form is the most precious dress of your soul.
To serve the suffering humanity, your steps must be
extraordinarily courageous and bold.

Quality of life depends upon
What you do, even if others don't know,
remember, you will reap only what you sow. !

LIVE TO LOVE

Live to love
rather than love to live.
Shun thoughts of getting something from someone,
instead, harbour thoughts to give.

Live and let live,
and, experience that bliss when, you unselfishly give.
Life is worth living.
This world is worth giving.

Live to give
even, your own life.
Loving poor, destitute and hapless
is worth a blissful strife.

Selfish love and living for self alone,

undoubtedly, makes anyone experience
a galore of moan and groan.

Alas ! everyone seems to live for self and none for others.
Why can't we all learn this blissful lesson from our mothers?

Her love is selfless and pure.
Her blessings; a blissful cure.

Other's life deserves love and respect.
Love alone can make your existence justified and perfect.
His entire creation is worth loving since He loves all.
Giving finishing touches to His glorious drama
is worth an effort rather than, we let it stall.

So, live to love without greed.
Love immensely without bothering about caste and creed.

Your genuine love will generate a chain reaction.
Tremendous energies thus released
will provide all a blissful protection.
Its the only way to kill
all kinds of germs of social, political and religious infection.

Try it and reinforce His benign glory.
You could surely provide that required healing touch
to this otherwise, awfully tragic story.

WISDOM

God has made none perfect,
not even, the majestic Peacock
who, looking at his legs & feet, gets a rude shock.

Had He done that, who would call Him
perfect ?
The realisation itself, makes one
remember Him with reverence as a matter of fact.

It's for us to realise our short comings
and then, make genuine efforts to over come.
That's how near perfection is achieved by some.
The sting in one's tongue & tail
Can bring about in one's life an unforgettable
storm & gale.
Vanity due to looks, physique, status, riches and wealth,
adversely effects psyche, life's freedom and general health.

Habit of telling lies,
makes one invariably cry and heave sighs.

A hypocrite, snooty and a show off is made out
and despised by all.
Complexes steal away One's strengths
and don't let one grow in real terms hefty and tall.

Innate goodness lies in correct self assessment and
evaluation.
Coupled with sincere and genuine efforts
without any inhibition and hesitation.

A WAY FOR SELF-IMPROVEMENT

True confession makes one feel light.
Coaxes thereafter, to do everything right.

Otherwise, guilt keeps bothering
both heart and mind.

It keeps eating up from within these
vital parts leaving absolutely sick mind behind.

If err is to human and forgive to divine,
Then, after committing a sin, it is
moral obligation to tell Him the
truth and seek His mercies and blessings benign.

Since, God is dealing with human
beings, He can possibly forgive
you once or twice.
Don't expect Him to care for you
if, you keep repeating sin and
reinforcing your vice.

It's a means to effect a dramatic
change of both heart & mind,
a practical way to convert your
savage psyche into a benevolent and kind.

Try it honestly, you may succeed.
Thereafter, to your inner voice, you've
to give due heed.

There's nothing wrong if you've committed a mistake.
Just make sure, you don't repeat
it for God's sake!

STRUGGLE FOR REAL FREEDOM

Where is my freedom gone
with which, I was born ?

Over the years, instead of consolidating, I lost it and

became a slave;
of egoism, lust, greed, pride, anger, jealousy and hate.

I may appear to some influential and rich
but, my slavery has made me spiritually a pauper.
So, I'll go through the rut most unnoticed
like on grass, a grass hopper.

I realise materialism is the root cause of this wretched
state.
The realisation itself, is undoubtedly rather late.

These forces have held me firmly in their yoke
and I'm left with a little time.
Towards my own soul, I've done a lot of crime.

Their target area is conscience which, is attacked
overwhelmingly from all directions.
Once penetrated, it gets extremely difficult
to offer meaningful resistance.

Materialism injects want, desire and crave.
These forces then, overpower conscience
and make anyone a nit-wit and naive.

Remedy lies in a relentless struggle
against the shackles of this worst form of slavery.
Thus, one can give oneself a good account of real bravery.

Will I die the death of a slave or will I be free
like, when I was born ?
Will I be able to get a hold on my conscience
or will it remain totally torn ?

THIS WORLD IS A PLAY-FIELD

I find almost everyone on the face of
our earth, playing games,
of course, under different names.

Some play in teams and some alone.
Any way, it doesn't matter as, all are
similar in their texture & tone.

Some follow unscrupulous but,
accepted rules and some, devise their own.
But, all aim to extract blood & sweat
of others, both known & unknown

Those, who think about their games as
totally Original are sadly mistaken.
As our ancestors also, knew
tastes of Ham & Bacon.

At the end of these games, some experience
delirium and some, transitory delights.
Soon to realise, that, only on empty and
meaningless aims had they focussed,
life long, their sights.

It's important and pertinent to ask
self a question; Towards pristine nature
and humanity, what's my contribution ?
If, an honest answer is nil then, rest assured,
God would feel sorry for affording you a unique chance
to be part of His incredibly fascinating creation !

FRIENDSHIP

They say 'a friend in need is a friend indeed'
and I say 'a true friend is one, who is friendly
both in thought and deed'.

To have a friend one has to be one.
For brightness, there has to be a visible sun.
A genuine friend would, both happiness & grief, share
and in these days are indeed very rare.

A friend you could find in anyone regardless of sex & age,
perhaps at any life's stage.

A good friend helps stabilise turbulent heart & mind.
helps set life's cruise on peaceful ways
leaving sordid past behind.

A sincere & honest friend is His one of worldly
ways of getting close
and making one sip a heavenly doze.

Those who have genuine friend's company,
find their life span as a very pleasant journey.

Yet, there's a friend always within,
whose friendship would keep you far away from all kinds of
sin.

He is ever ready to listen to your woes & sighs.
To be with Him, you've to just call for Him after
closing your eyes.

Try Him once and give Him a genuine try.
I'm sure, your genuine effort would put an end to all your
cry !

A LINK BETWEEN PAST AND FUTURE

Like sea is sometimes calm and some times rough,
So is life, which is, one day,
smooth and another day rather tough.
What's going to happen is always a great mystery.
At the end of it, people term it a part of history.

Rather than one's future, present is most important.
Only lessons of the past are however, sacrosanct.

Present makes one's would be past and future good or bad.
Present would determine whether one would turn out to be a gentleman or a cad.

Present is nothing, but what you think and act.
Cumulative effect of you action, which is your present, makes past and future as a matter of fact.

Thinking about future without putting in earnest effort, is inviting frustration and despair.
Whereas, being sincere in thought and action is rather fair.

Generally, success kisses feet of those who dare.
Therefore, management of anyone's present, needs utmost care.

Life goes on from one moment to another, which is present.
Therefore, each moment if gainfully spent, can make entire life span rather pleasant.

What was one's present once upon a time, is now one's past.
Remember, future is, what one's present would cast.

PERSEVERANCE AND PATIENCE

Like a spring, beginning of all big things is rather small.
Like everyone before walking, learns to crawl.

Like a rain drop is very much part of an ocean.
Soul of every living being is in essence the same one God in motion.

It descends into and ascends out of any one, at His will.
Rest is all a mere common story of someone in a typical mill.

We forget that this Universe for it's present existence has taken billions of years.
Spirit and Cultural heritage of any race is outcome of cumulative efforts of countless philosophers, thinkers, sages and seers.

Like construction of house takes time, while it's destruction, comparatively nil.
In happiness, times fly while in despair, it seems stand still.

Those, who aspire to get to dizzy heights in the twinkling of an eye, obviously live in fools paradise.
However, those who believe in the maxim of "Slow and Steady wins the race" are undoubtedly wise.

Those, who are sincere about their goal, burn midnight oil, while their contemporaries sleep.
When you lose sight of the very aim, you can land up in trouble, sometimes, unmanageable and deep.

Genuine efforts and patience alone, can ensure tranquillity of mind.

Remember, after testing you alone, would He be, benevolent and kind !

KEEP YOUR KITE FLYING

In my childhood, kite flying was more than an obsession,
I used to dream about in my class-rooms about the evening session.

It was my ardent desire to be the best in kite flying.
Obviously, it required expert hands and real professional and business like buying.

I realized whenever my thread was weak and full of knots,
I lost my kites by the dozen and was a laughing stock of even tiny tots.

With frail thread, kite couldn't remain intact due to velocity of strong breeze,
whereas, light and small kites would, with those gushes, just freeze.

Now, I realise how true it is to life ;
knotty, twisted, and weak characters, can't brave rough times and put up with strife.

Kite of life, soon gets severed.
Thereafter, drifts away in a manner, uncontrolled and weird.
So, if keeping your life-kite up, above all, is your exciting quest.
Remember, thread of strong, straight and uncompromising character is the best bet !

POSITIVITY IN LIFE

I get fascinated when I behold;
On a tree, squirrels playing hide and seek,
mother bird back on her nest with an insect in her beak.
team of climbers with their flag right on top of a virgin peak.

Ants sharing mammoth weight.
Crocodile's rocking tongue as a bait.
Tiger next to a water point hiding in wait,
Teenager awaiting impatiently for his date,

Amidst murky mud, a full bloom lotus flower,
upon dry and hot sand dune, a torrential shower,
On a historical battlefield, a victory tower.

Worker bee's devotion towards their Queen bee,
dextrous hands in a tea garden plucking tea,
undaunting determination of sea divers rummaging a
mighty sea.

Pet dog's faithfulness and devotion,
Peacock's dance sequence and majestic motion.
Beaming and radiant face of someone returning home with
promotion.

Soldiers fighting their way into enemy lines.
newly born calf, before walking, stumbling on hoofs many
times.
Mountain slopes studded with rows of pines
Infant's expressions on the sight of his mother.

about a grown up sister, the concerned looks of a big
brother.

Mother Teresa's feeling on the sufferings of other.

Rain and sun together, falling on a patch.

Team's, hugs and kisses to the player who was instrumental in winning a tough fought match,
Expressions of a fisherman on realisation of his unimaginable catch.

I, also, get fascinated with the ups and downs of life.
My fascination propels me to cope up smilingly with the privations and sufferings which are, more than rife.

Managers must draw their own practical lessons while observing Mother-nature.
Remember, only those, who, analyse the forces of pure love, devotion, unflinching faith and determination can hope to improve upon meaningfully their stature !

YOU CAN CALL SHOTS

When one loses the basic will to live,
rest assured, thereafter, for this world, one is left with nothing to give.

People experience that because of total disenchantment, realizing the realities of life with disillusionment.

Therefore, the number of remaining breaths is any one's guess.
In fact, some await impatiently the blessed time which is to put an end to this veritable mess.

Life goes on as long as there is will.
Like, without breeze the atmosphere will be still.

Some say at the time of retirement from their job, that they are sick of work and need rest,
and only attend to mundane house-hold chores or attend to garden at best.
Soon, they realize that they run out of their zest.
Time then disdainfully lingers on.
Moments turn out to be years and somehow usher in after each night, yet another stereotyped dawn.
Thus, one is bound to leave this world in misery.
As, before finally putting down shutters, mind flashes back all weired images of the sordid life history.

Life regardless of it's span, is worth, if, it's with a noble purpose or aim.
Without which, all your excuses to justify your life events are more than lame.

A noble cause will keep you energized with a will to go on.
At the end of it, there would be happiness, smiles, cheers, celebrations and jubilations and so forth and so on.

WAY TO SUCCESS

Act fearlessly.
Argue logically.
Behave nicely.
Communicate clearly.

Dress smartly.
Earn honestly.
Give generously.
Handle tactfully.

Judge impartially.
Manage appropriately.

Pay promptly.
Risk cautiously.
Spend intelligently.
Think constructively.
Serve willingly.
Invest prudently.
Listen attentively.
Observe curiously.
Admonish privately.
Reward publicly.
Question cleverly.
Read vivaciously.
Tell briefly.
Work efficiently.
Bottom line is, for meaningful success, sincerity of thought and purpose is a must.
Remember, first is always first !

ANALYSIS AND EVALUATION

Despite ice caps at both ends, earth's core is red hot
Like the inside and outside of a filled up clay tea pot.

Cursed are those who are chicken hearted and are as good or bad as living dead.

Blessed are those who by hard work and perserverance earn their own bread.

Imbalanced ones, blow hot and cold in the same breath

Unstable are those, who unnecessarily worry about their future and death.

Those who are vicious and malicious, despite exotic perfumes, putrefy the heavens.

Amidst countless stars above us, universal truth ; True North is indicated by the "Great Sevens".

Earthen pitchers keep water cool even when they brave a hot sun.

Not withstanding rank, status and influence all would reduce to just dust and ashes after it is all done !

Lucky are those, who, know how to control internal and external heat.

Really healthy are those, who, maintain a cool head on warm feet.

IMPORTANCE OF RISK TAKING

How, where and when are you going to breathe last is slated for you before your come into this form.

Then, why on earth, are you scared and worried about man-made tempests and storm ?

Life without risk is as good as dead.
It's this risk taking alone, which, would make you use you head.

Those who risk, display ample faith both in self and God.
Passive life whereas, is, as ungracious as a reluctant nod.

Flow in life is inherent as that in river.
Both go together like chill and shiver.

Body and mind must be put to test, lest they rust.
Excitement and satisfaction must be experienced before merging with dust !

Only those, who dare and risk,
leave their name and chivalrous stories behind.
Therefore, one has to prepare to steel up one's psyche and mind;
to accept roughs of life with smile and grace
and dare to accept all kinds of risks of a real hot chase.

Mental and physical toughness comes with a strong and stout heart.
Therefore, it does matter which is before, horse or the cart!

As and when, one tries to put an artificial block to natural flow of life,
ugly manifestations of curbed and curtailed flow, would add hardships manifold to one's otherwise normal strife.

Those, who, surrender to circumstances,
lose honour too in addition to their lives.
Remember, a diver can only
fathom the depth, only after he dives !

HUMOROUS APPROACH

Humour in life comes out of positive approach, wit and wisdom.
It's a sure way to kill emptiness, disinterest and boredom.
Those, who, receive it's daily dose,
are able to face this world with a straight nose.

Through humour, one can soften the hard blows of life.

With laughter, heart remains tension-free through hard moments of strife.

Remember, laughter reduces mental distance between even worst of foes.
Quite funny is the link between one's heels and toes.

It's a skill that, one can acquire with ease.
After acquisition, nurturing it, would, bring in your life real peace.

Through laughter alone, you could survive most painful situation
like, any written expression would become meaningful, only after application of right kind of punctuation.

Laughter is a barometer of anyone's general health.
It just can't be compensated by worldly riches or wealth.

We are here for only a short spell, so how about laughing a while !
Rather than anger, let a fit of laughter now and then, sans the vile !

A FUTILE EFFORT

It's nice not to know what is in store
Otherwise, life'd have been such a bore !

Hope, aspirations and efforts are synonym of life.
That's how, anyone, gets geared up to put up with strife.

If a man knows accurately what's ahead.
From then onwards, he's as good or bad as dead.

Charm of life lies in ignorance about future.

Those who try and find out, only, attempt to tamper with life's natural flow and culture.

If life is action,
future is, as a result of reaction.

Remember action and reaction are always equal and opposite.
Present and future are integrated package; thoroughly composite.

In order to alter course of events, people wear many a stone,
shear and grind as part of 'black magic' many a rare bone.

To have a genuine realistic aspiration, dedicated effort and leaving results to Him is the most practical way.
That's how, in materialistic world, one can hopefully be peaceful and happily stay.

Man, who, unnecessarily worries and harbours fearful apprehensions about future, portraits a weak-kneed tottering personality. Actually, he needs to develop self confidence, optimism and faith in self and whole humanity.

ONE IS NEVER TOO LATE

Everyone is here on the face of earth just for sometime.
It is up to us to go on doing good to others or keep committing against one self and others misdeeds and crime after crime.

It is entirely our own choice.
i.e., either to listen world's decibles or own inner voice.

Easiest course is to be selfish and forget the rest.

Who choses the harder right than easier wrong obviously, clears the ring-test.

Remember, nobody is going to miss you when you aren't here.

This world, without you also, would go on in the same gear.

Quality of your life depends on what you think and act
Real happiness or sorrow follows each such act as a matter of fact.

Number of dots constitute a straight line.
Similarly, on number of predetermined breaths depends a life-time.

Bitter truth is that no one is sure of one's next breath.
and also, number and forms of lives after death.

If it's so, why are we groping in dark ?
When will we consider and accept selfless service as our life's quality hall-mark ?

Sooner the better.
Otherwise, our dreams would never get transformed into reality and our empire at the end of our play in front of our own eyes, would, just mercilessly shatter.

Therefore, do it just now
and ponder about only ways and means i.e. how ?

TICKLE ANYONE WITHOUT TOUCH

A smile costs nothing but, gives so much.
It tickles onlookers without the physical touch.

It enriches those who receive without making poorer those who give.

Makes one realise how to live.

It takes only a moment but, the memory of it sometimes, lasts for ever.
Helps win over enemies and even the over-clever.

None is so rich or mighty that he can get along without it, none is so poor that he can't be made rich by it.

A smile creates happiness in the home, fosters goodwill in business and promotes friendship.
It's implicit and natural response foster meaningful fellowship.

It is nature's best antidote for troubled and worried mind and brings sunshine to the sad, cheer to discouraged and rest to someone under a draconic grind.

Some people are too sick to give you a smile and carry a stern face,
give them one of your's as they seem to have already lost their life's race.

This small curve on your face can straighten out many things.
The receiving mind shuns mental blocks, angularities and kinks.

Remember, a put on smile is ungraceful and infact, an insult
Rather than generating pleasant feelings, it causes hurt.

A smile bridges all mental barriers
Therefore, for the good of man-kind, let us all be at least genuine smile carriers !

WE CAN DO IT

We must wonder to realise all wonderful things around us.
We must marvel to comprehend all marvellous things of our universe.

We must seek and see beauty to realise beautiful creations.
We must fathom the creator's magnanimity, benevolence, unlimited potential for our recreation.

To realise, His blessings, we must serve selflessly to find real happiness and joys.
We must sieve the actual from worldly decoys.

We must know unambiguously what's good and what's bad for our planet and whole universe.
Otherwise, we'll keep hurling upon each other abuses and curse.

Our suffocations and choke points are our self-created pseudo lines of divisions.
Basically, because of our parochial visions.

Let us live every moment and promote healthy and happy life as much as we can.
Let there be universal bondage of brotherhood between man and another man.

Our children today, hear perpetually distinct noises of hate and anger everywhere.
What will they become in due course ? We need to take care.

Life in any form around us responds warmly to genuine

love, care and affection.

Fundamentally, in this thought alone, lies the Universal key to end all self-created pain and suffocation.

Let us all smell and appreciate roses as we all go along. Rather than, looking at thorns and keep doing only wrong.

Let us all shake up our heads, clear our visions and focus our collective wisdom for the common good of all man-kind. and having done our bit, leave for our children, crops of unfathomable joy and pleasures behind ! We can do it !

ALL IS UP TO YOU

Your eyes would see with due training and practice what you want them to see.
Your mind would be what you want it to be.

Beauty lies in the eyes of a beholder and so does vulgarity and obscenity.
Harmonious heart, mind and soul see and appreciate every where His artistry and creativity.

Worldly materialistic dust is like haze,
ever causing, dilution to our gaze.

There is need to have clear vision more than ever before as, suffocating and choking complex materialistic blizzards are causing eye-sore.

The magnitude of the vision depends upon the power of light that shines within.
Clarity of picture would depend upon the degree of faith in self and in Him !

AN ABSOLUTE TRUTH

People visit temples and mosques to be with Him
not realizing, that, He resides all the time within.

People visit shrines to get His personal care
whereas, only inner voice with their mind, they, need to
share.

People follow meaningless religious customs, dogmas,
rituals and ceremonies aimed to placate Him
not realizing that, all these are a big waste of money and
time as through these, prospects of achieving the aim are
absolutely slim.

Some pose to be close to Him and appear to the world as
saints and sages.
On innocent God fearing people, who, visit to pay their
respects, they cast treacherous, malicious and swindler's
gazes.

If you want to live with Him, there is no need to go
anywhere.
Dive deep into inner depths and explore your inner World
and then feel His personal company in His true form
thread-bare.

He is so near that anyone can see Him
regardless whether lights are full or dim.

One can feel his gracious presence at all times everywhere
since He resides within.
In this life, there can't be a better friend or relative than
Him.

WE SHOULD KNOW THAT

If we make our bodies abode of pure thoughts and actions, we would automatically establish our rapport with outside world through very healthy and purposeful interactions.

No man has ever got lost on a straight road.
That's the surest way to avoid carrying on our heads at all times, tons of load.

Outstanding people have one thing in common ; an absolute sense of mission.
Instead of confrontation, in confronting the problem, lies the solution.

When we choose to be pleasant and positive in the way we treat others.
We, then, also choose in most cases, how we're going to be treated by others.

Harmony and inner peace is to be found in following scrupulously a moral compass that points in the same direction regardless of what people say.
One becomes great by doing small things in a great way.

Our interactions & conversations with people, leave good or bad tastes behind.

Everytime we open our mouth, we let people look into our mind.

Men and women are limited not by the place of their birth, not by the colour of their skin, but by the size of their hope.
Good leaders inject their led with pragmatic hope.

It is more noble to love the person next to us than it is to love in general, the mankind.

One's actions are directly proportional to what one feeds one's mind.

Effectiveness is doing the right thing and, efficiency is doing things right.

The ladder of success works like any other ladder.

Very few, with their hands in pockets have climbed any meaningful height.

Courage is not the absence of fear;
it is going ahead despite the fear.

When we turn to God, we discover He has been facing us all the time.

Fear of a sinner is, in itself, a crime.

The 'free cheese' is in a mousetrap.

He alone can bestow upon anyone heaps of pleasures & happiness in a split second straight in one's lap.

The best thing a parent can do for a child is to love his or her spouse.

Unselfish love, compassion, understanding and trust can only bring happiness in any house.

When you break goals into increments and start controlling your time, light of success begin to appear.

Even on the road to success, one has to halt to take stock of things till one gets, the signal of 'all clear'.

Kids go where there's excitement however, they stay, where there's love both by night and day.

They pay more attention to what you do than what you say.

When a job is loved, work makes life sweet, meaningful and full of gratitude.
Maintaining the right attitude is easier than regaining the right attitude.

If you learn from a defeat, you haven't really lost.
When you compromise with your self respect and dignity, you do it at unimaginable cost.

Hands that serve humanity are a lot better than lips that talk of divinity.
On the sands of time, foot prints of leaders who live and die with honour, remain till eternity.

Intoxication decreases inhibitions
but, increases exhibitions.

Best way to have a genuine friend is to be one.
Friendship between two selfless friends would last till the great Sun.

LIFE WITH REAL BLISS AND JOY

Joy lies behind each creation and therefore, living and dissolving in joy is everyone's natural birth right.
But, what a pity, for most of us, neither through life nor at the end of it, real joy is ever in sight.

Devilish man finds joy in destruction.
An athlete finds it through his physical power expression.

Artist achieves it through creative and higher reflections.
Whereas, a scientist's joy lies in unraveling mysteries of nature and her deflections.

Undoubtedly, there is no joy equal to the one, which comes by through selfless service and action.

Only those, who, live with the motto of 'Service Before Self' can get sucked into the blissful field of real joy and genuflection.

Attainment of true knowledge of life ushers analloyed joys. Only those, who, know "why" before knowing "how" can see through worldly materialistic decoys !

While, frustration and dejection are unmistakable signs of lack of shaky confidence.

Tackling the root-cause positively and pragmatically reflects mind's resilience and brilliance.

TENSION FREE LIFE

Tension is due to misdeeds,
Like crops are due to their seeds.

Ill got is generally, ill spent,
like a tenant who ends up paying either voluntarily or by a court order, his rent.

We don't think before doing a wrong.
Thereafter, we keep hearing day in and day out sounds of danger bells and gong.

Even, if, wrong remains unnoticed, one gets older faster.
Since, One doesn't have any longer that privilege of having a carefree and natural laughter.

Tension free life alone, could be healthy,
One without tension, could only be really wealthy.

Going against established norms, customs and rules for personal gains is a sure path leading to enormous mental agony and pain.
Some, thus, due to accumulated stress, end up as insane.

Only, clean and right dealings can keep you absolutely dry even in incessant rain.
Our actions san conscience are undoubtedly, our biggest bane.

To me, everyone seems to live in a glass-house.
Whenever, one's pants are down,
On-lookers exclaim, What a louse !

Even if others don't see, at least,
you know for sure, what you are.
That keeps on nagging and thus,
all happiness of life, you yourself mar.

Abide by rules, norms, customs and have fair dealings.
Remember, in your old house, you can't remain protected for long by only false ceilings !

When you look at yourself in the mirror each morning, you should be able to look in your eyes.
You could do that only if you hadn't been telling lies.

Happiness from within is, in life, everyday's sun-shine.
This is something that one just can't purchase anywhere with any amount of dime.

❑

3

PRACTICAL
LIFE
MANAGEMENT

TIME MANAGEMENT

Amongst all the resources of management, the most precious one is time.
To kill it or while it away is, undoubtedly, the biggest crime.

Those managers, who, value it right from the word "GO", are on the right track.
Those, who, ignore it's value, are destined to get a sack.

It must be realized that time once lost is lost for ever.
It's apt utilisation for best resultant advantage, is, a move rather professional and clever.

Time is wealth.
It's right appreciation and right prioritisation would, dictate any organisation's health.

Time management, a manager must, as part of his second nature,
Creation of value-based time-utility, ethos and culture would enhance any manager's stature.

Our mother-nature handles time in natural life cycles in a very deft manner.
Time-utility managers only, are, likely to carry here after, successful organisation's banner.

Time management for self and for society, one has to start at an early age.
Life is too short and one only realises this truth at a very late stage.

Then, there is no use crying over spilt milk.
Remember, in an ill-timed sericulture farm, one can't hope

to get good quality-silk!

A meticulous time plan and its prioritisation, for any success, is an essential pre-requisite.
Only deep knowledge and it's practice could enable any manager to figure out a workable plan; par-exquisite.

Time utility managers, in due course, develop a knack of converting time at hand into a valuable asset
and then, in execution stage, convert odds and disadvantages into advantages with zeal and zest.

Ancient Hindus revered time as one of their Gods, regulating their life-span in a dynamic and powerful way.
They had devised many a scientific technique to manage each breath (unit measure of life time) both by night and day.

Each breath, when managed to it's optimum degree, ensures long life and a great health.
That's why, Yogis, Rishis and Munis lived hundreds and thousands of years defying time and offered in person to many a generation, pure Gyana; the knowledge-wealth.

According to Indian scriptures, Time is Destroyer as well as a great Creator.
It is destined to destroy even the Universe in this marvellous cosmic theatre.

In the ultimate analysis, all known successful men of our world, had managed this great resource most efficiently.
That's how exactly, we, could, too, manage this scarce resource (comparatively short-life span) most proficiently.

DECISION MAKING AND THEREAFTER

Unless you admit, acknowledge and pause,
how can you hope to get at the real cause ?

Any live situation merits understanding the verticals and horizontals, as then alone, a worth-while picture would emerge.

Otherwise, it would remain incomprehensible, lop-sided or veiled behind a surge.

Application of common sense, logic and experience would then, help you weigh various pros and cons.
Remember, you can only tame a bull, when, you hold him by his horns.

Mental block or a bias causes 'Analysis Paralysis'
which, in turn, leads one to a state of 'Decision Paralysis'.

This disease, either delays decision or makes it unsound.
As a result, one instead of heading straight out for destination, goes, spinning around.

At the same time, any action without due thought is a sheer waste of time.
Whereas, slothfulness and procrastination, itself, is, towards own self, a serious crime.

Decision, therefore, has to be timely and sound.
Otherwise, logically, any project may not even take off ground.

Once, you've reached a decision, you must go full steam.
Keep your eyes and ears open as you go along and don't you get into a day dream.

Application of correction is more than vital
like, ascribing a poem, it's apt title.

You would encounter challenges ; both pseudo and formidable.
Keep your wits cool and intact without being brash and irritable.

Don't blame anyone, even, luck for a failure and keep cribbing.
Sometimes, goal isn't scored, as there had been too much of unnecessary dribbling.

Success in any venture is sum total of everything.
put in including "General Luck".
Remember, sometimes even first class world cricketers, get out at "duck".

Those, who arrive at decision, and act,
find themselves certainly better than indecisive one's infact.

Success, however, in no way, should swell up your head.
If it's so, you're as good as living dead.

RELATIONSHIP MANAGEMENT

Right from our enterance into this world till our exit from it, rarely we're alone.
In-fact, whole life consists of series of interactions with people ; known, not so known and even unknown.

While the need to interact with others, is inescapable,
this other, as friend or foe, lover or mate, parent or child, employer or servant, senior or subordinate is inevitable.

These interactions, whether brief or long-lasting, are relationships.

These usher in our lives both joys and hard-ships.

Without an appreciative partner with whom to share our lives, the glory of riches, of fame, of achievement fades to dust and ashes.

That's why, longing and search for this special person goes on while wearing all our caps and sashes.

Most of our relationships are due to chance while, some significant ones are our own choice.

In the selection of our parents, siblings, children, co-workers or neighbours, obviously we've no voice.

Rarely are our relationships due to objective forethought. Even those, who'are close to us, have usually come to us through some fortunate twist of fate that places them on our path.

In fact, interaction with others takes much of our energy and fills our working hours with a myriad of emotions and thought.

In it's wake, due to our own perceptions, as we sail through our days, we experience joys and sorrows as our lot.

Sometimes, relationships can prove far stronger than either individual leading us to believe that a certain kind of 'Synergy' is at work.

Many a times before getting into relationships, thoughts about the would be relationship-potential on our minds, lurk.

Sometimes it is possible that our sub-conscious minds are

sufficiently sophisticated to know on a very subtle level, what's the relation-ship-potential even as our eyes, first time meet.

In fact, on such occasions, two pairs of eyes recognizing well this potential, in a unique and mystic manner greet.

Positive, creative, unselfish, healthy and progressive interactions make us the experience most ecstatic joys and unfathomable pleasures.

While, the negative, uncreative, selfish, unhealthy and regressive interactions give us the experience of greatest sorrows beyond any measures.

One is required to give up individual ego in service of the relationship.

Remember, if one is in it for what one can get, it would lead to meaningless effort culminating into hard-ship.

Kindness, understanding, trust and consideration are worth more than all the selfish pleasures you can gain.

In respecting your partner's space, listening to him or her and truly sharing with him or her, there is no scope for anyone to experience any shame.

Working out differences through calm discussion is often the best way.

You may agree to disagree but can't afford to wake up with violent disagreements on each new day.

Beware of possessiveness and claiming behaviour as this would amount to treating your partner as an object or possession.

Remember, in making a valued relationship tick, there is no

room for falsehood and pretension.

Learn to postpone your gratification through patience, understanding and trust.

In the service of relationship, giving unconditionally is a must.

Relationships nurtured with utmost sincerity of heart and mind,

would, undoubtedly fill up life with nostalgic memories rather than many a heartache and grind.

Rather than 'me & me', one needs to work for 'you and me' equation.

That alone could ensure in life, plenty of joy, happiness and elation.

LIVE EVERYDAY

Life isn't a bed of roses,

Occasionally, you keep getting happy and unhappy doses.

When times are bad, you plunge into
unfathomable depths of despair,
start saying every moment 'I don't care.'

On every happening, you seek in utter disgust, explanations.

What others are doing then, are your only attractions.

On every conceivable misfortune, you start saying 'why me'?

Egoism fattens your head and you feel that for all locks, only you, possess the key.

You get more bothered about what others will say,
keep thinking only of your past day.

All this is bound to take you nowhere
except, amidst ever increasing frustration, disgust and
despair.

Thus, you invite yourself
unnecessary and uncalled for strife.
All this affects your love, children and family life.

You can effect a dramatic change without a sweat.
Honestly, it is without fume and fret.

When comfronted with an awkward one,
have a put on smile.
Be calm even if he stirs up his bile.

Don't you ever jump to conclusions
as you'll often frighten the best ones away.
Even amidst the worst, count His blessings
and learn to be carefree both by night and day.

If you visit a surgical ward, orphanage and cremation
grounds once a week, you'll never go wrong.
These would have such a sublime effect
that you'll be really happy life long.

Simplicity, honesty and truthfulness
will make you a darling of all.
Remember, life is a soccer game in which, you have to
somehow, make sure that you alone have a solid hold on
the ball.

SUCCESS MANAGEMENT

Most of us think that one is successful if one makes a lot of money.
So that, one could do what one wants to and experience each & every day as bright and sunny.

More, than half of these so called successful men's life is spent in collecting dimes at the cost of their own health.
And then, the remaining life is spent in getting health alright by paying up major part of their accumulated wealth.

Because of attachment with wealth,
when you lose it, you again get ill health.

Thus, this vicious cycle goes on for sometime till it comes to an abrupt end
what a pity, the so-called successful man doesn't get time to even mend or relent.

In any case, nothing goes along.
Even most successful man forsakes any claim on his money when death sounds it's gong.

Success means happiness and constant inner peace
where in, deep longings, yearnings and desires to make somehow money just cease.

Most of our activities are meaningless and worthless as the motivation behind is only self-interest.
BeCause only self reigns supreme deep beneath our chest.
That's why, we remain engrossed in working and figuring out what's for self and near and dear one's the best.

That's exactly where we go wrong

and, waste this precious life just for a mythical song.

Management for success in life lies in righteous actions spirited by inner voice.
Therefore, fathoming and exploiting our inner potentials for our activities in the outer world should be our only choice.

WAY TO PEACEFUL LIFE

Rarely have I come across a happy and contented man in life.
Despite materialistic pleasures, rich accumulated religious experience of forefathers, his life is full of mental agony and strife.

What's that bothers man today, and causes
within him vibrations other than those of peace and bliss ?
It's undoubtedly a subject of genuine concern to
all mankind worth a kiss.

Today, man really can't be blamed for his values and their emptiness.
Since his childhood, he's been taught to appreciate things unrelated to truth and real happiness.

It's high time to realise that we have become
victims of our own values and state of mind.
That's why, we leave the pristine divine happiness,
that all of us experience in our childhood, far behind.

We don't realize that how we live is important
and not how long is this life.
We get engrossed with only materialistic strife.

We busy ourselves with temples, mosques and

religious ceremonies to heap His love without loving His creation.

We busy ourselves with numerous pleasure hunts and drives not knowing that they are poor substitutes for happiness and lead us to frustration.

We busy ourselves in getting entangled in the silky webs of cosmic delusions turning deaf ears
to inner promptings.
Yet, at the end, all of us expect from this
meaningless life a purposeful ending !

And, we busy ourselves in working for own glamour and glory totally forgetting that of God.
Busy ourselves in attaining greater materialistic heights without conquering 'self Lord.'

As a result, man leaves this world crying the way he came
Then, his soul wanders pitifully in His 84 lakh forms of creation frame.

God has given us sight to see His greatness and
mind to understand Him.
Sight helps in realising His existence and mind in finding Him.

The cosmic delusions only attack the mind and
impair its comprehension and judgements.
Anger, greed, pride and attachment are thus
the natural increments.

Our pride, pseudo-egoism and expectations go beyond our logic.
They torment and stifle our hearts and minds and turn the

story tragic.

Haven't we suffered enough by going along
the ways of the so called civilized world ?
It's high time we retire to the world within us,
which, speaks a language altogether different.

As years go by, everyone seems to be growing only in age,
his selfishness and pride get him pity and unusual rage.
He doesn't listen to the promptings of the genuine
friend within his body cage.
At the fag end, deceits self by behaving like pseudo sage.

By identifying with the Ocean, a drop of water becomes
part of it, otherwise, it would stand isolated and without any
stature.
We'll begin to experience many wonderful moments of
fantasy and blissful joy once we've identified with nature.

When the going is bad, even own shadows disappear.
When it's good, unheard people as near and dear from
nowhere, appear.

All materialistic relations are false.
It's a reality rather harsh.

Undoubtedly, the ways to wealth are many but to
universal truth only one which, lies beyond our selfish
pursuit.
Truth is reality, reality God, God purity and
from purity comes feelings without which, man is a big fool.

It is hope which lies at the heart of all creations,
and it's this hope, which is source of all
distress, despair and frustration.

Expectations in life bring invariably misery and gloom.
Shed it off and expect nothing from any one, not
even from your own body & live with the strength of your
soul and then experience the same life without a groan.

If you can slash hope and desire,
there is no difference between you and your creator.
There is a unique pleasure in sharing our joys with other.

It is only then, life appears meaningful and
brings in it's fold a purposeful death.
Otherwise, it is just another heap of breath over breath.

Let inner vibrations take over your head and heart
and goad you to do good.
Your actions will let you experience unfathomable
pleasures as much as you could.

Count His blessings by visiting orphanage and
hospital once a day,
feel the change in you and see your life turning gay.

For peace and stability, nothing like temperance;
It's a magic key to life full of roses and fragrance.

Unless one is tuned with inner-self and live
a peaceful life within,
It's a sheer waste and whole life stinks like an unattended
garbage bin.

Unless one is in complete control of self with
unflinching faith and firm resolve,
life will remain mysteriously dark and this riddle,
man, unable to solve.

YOU DESERVE A BREAK

Day to day life chores make one's
life awfully busy,
so much so, that one often feels dizzy.

They say change of work and
routine has inherent rest,
still, one has to keep
always, a watch on sagging zeal and zest.

Life without interest and 'go'
tires one rather fast,
result is stress, strain and fatigue
which, doesn't let one last.

Therefore, off and on, one needs a break.
Sometimes, even for just heck of it sake.

You must go out of your
house for enjoying a week end,
with people whom you love and
admire e.g. your wife, sons,
daughters and genuine friend.

It is a must to behave like
a child or go crazy once a while.
Be cheerful and have a free and natural
laughter and always bear your charming smile.

During the day, find sometime to hear or
tell an anecdote.
Be romantic in your thoughts & keep riding
that life's fun boat.

During week days sometimes,
have a break and call up
someone who is dear.
Try and brave a pleasant
smile in your place of work for all far and near.

Don't you bother unnecessarily about, what will
people talk,
life, would then appear, a cake walk.

TRAINEE IS MANAGER'S CHILD

Training any trainee for a manager is, like teaching own
child.
Therefore, in so doing, his innovative and creative skills
must be encouraged to run wild.

The standard and quality of training will dictate the end
product.
Like, the sharpness and ferocity of cutting by the saw would
decide the quality and quantity of saw-dust.

A manager must prepare under-trainee's mind ready to
learn
and ever-ready, in pursuit of excellence, let his energies
burn.

Take pains in teaching him, what he is required to do in
reality
and make him inquisitive and desirous enough in equipping
self in chosen field of learning, a super-speciality.

Teach him tricks of the trade as much as you can
but in so doing, also develop him into a compassionate,

mature, and a caring man.

He should be trained in the actual conditions in which later on he is likely to perform his job.
That's the way to help and save him from many a sigh and sob.

Knowledge, experience, motivation and teaching skills of a teacher provide the requisite atmosphere and thrust.
Remember, that unbreakable bond between a trainer and trainee is based on mutual reverence and trust !

DEATH MANAGEMENT

Death denotes end of life's one phase.
It only ushers one in another form over a different stage.

God's own spark in us; soul (Atma) is a highly concentrated cosmic energy which can never become dead and cold.
It adorns different available dresses and costumes when it is fed up with the old.

Therefore, the phenomenon of death is a welcome milestone.
Change is always for the better as, it reinforces life's lustre, texture and tone.

There is no point in ever dreading death as it has to happen.
Therefore, don't waste your breath and let your spirits dampen.

Peaceful death is a sign of fulfilment.
Death, for a noble cause is a divine achievement.

To be peaceful at one's last, one has to be honest to self and to Him all throughout.
Killing one's conscience is a cowardly death each time, and in that, let there be no doubt.

Remember, this inevitable phenomenon at least once a day.
The thought of it, would make you evaluate your ends and means and consequently mend your way.

Death management is an every day affair.
It involves conscientious and gracious living amidst healthy air.

It's effective management would make you laugh at death, and in the process, you would derive utmost satisfaction and happiness out of each breath.

A LEADER MUST

Value and appreciate what one has
rather than what others have.

Appear, work and behave in a dignified manner at all times.
And shun the company, no matter how influential, of those, who, indulge in crimes.

Have the inner courage and conviction to stand up for what's morally right.
And when all other means are exhausted, be prepared to pick up sword and fight.

Lead the led from the front and set an example worth emulation.
Have a cheerful and gracious disposition amidst crisis, as

if, amidst celebration and jubilation.

Keep his calm and cool even amidst greatest of provocation.
Follow the dictates of his conscience without any second thought or hesitation.

Never part with wit, subtle humour and wisdom.
Rather than outer, be interested in expanding the boundaries of inner kingdom.

Win the hearts and minds by respect, love and affection.
Deal with subordinates with tenets of 'No nonsence' and gracious benevolence and compassion.

Follow himself what he preaches and teach.
Have requisite faith in self and all the humanity within reach.

Surrender to circumstances and results beyonds one's control.
Do righteous acts and strive to achieve desired results by yolking together heart and soul.

Give generously the credit of success to the led.
And amidst praise, not ever have a swollen head.

Respect his seniors and elders in a gracious way.
Act boldly backed by conscience, and not ever give vent to the thought; 'What others will say ?'

Consider leading a rare and sacred privilege and His most benign gift.
And, in the pursuit of excellence, not waiver, shift or drift.

WINDS OF CHANGE

Man is generally averse and sometimes repulsive to change,
yet, it's the only phenomenon due to which, man has since "Stone Age", done things more than strange.

Gigantic multidimensional winds of change are now sweeping the whole world.
Internationalisation and globalisation of market is inducing a fierce competition hitherto unheard.

Age-old dead enemies are today on honey moon.
Trade, commerce and market economic field would be the new battlefields soon.

Erstwhile enemies have no longer deadly weapon systems aimed at each other.
In the euphoria of war for universal peace, each one is behaving like a good brother.

Quantity with quality in trade and commerce is the order of the day.
Plan globally, think regionally and act locally, the corporate planners all over the world, now say.

The whole world is considered now as one market
International corporate planners don't ever keep all their eggs in one basket.

It is essential to have the right man at the right spot. doing, the right job in right way at right time.
There is seasoned professional approach for everything, even towards crime.

Days of prediction and certainty in business are on decline. Complexity, uncertainty, challenges, threats and constraints on the minds of decision-makers are at all time.

Survivability depends on who can forsee opportunity and is ready to grab,
and constantly engage with it, with all energies, rather than after a success, be complacent and brag.

Communist Germans and capitalist Germans have broken down with their own hands the dividing wall.
South African Cricketeers are now all over the world with their bat and ball.

Whole world is becoming aware of the need of ecological balance.
Keeping our planet green is one great and formidable challenge.

Let us remove poverty, illiteracy and religious fanaticism from the face of our earth,
and usher in meaningful peace and prosperity for each 'n' everyone on our only one common hearth !

BE A MAN

Those, who, in moments of crisis,
bite their nail,
in trying times, turn pale,
don't face up a gale,
& are always seen wagging
their tail,
certainly, aren't worth

being called a male.

Those, who, possess courage
of conviction, are
really great.
Greatest is he, who,
doesn't compromise it
for any bait.

Some don't mind paying,
for calling spade a spade,
any price,
like a bread is to be
knifed in order to
get a slice.

Life is worth living if
you bring courage into it.
Those, who, surrender, lose
honour too, in addition to
their lives with it.

People recall memories of those
who exhibited dauntless
courage with reverence.
Those who live and die with courage,
certainly deserve both
friend's & foe's due deference.

TRAINING OF MIND

Thoughts keep raking man's mind
leaving disturbing ripples and commotion behind.

Stone thrown in a pond disturbs it's peace and tranquillity.
Similarly, thought disturbs mind's cool and serenity.

Good and benign thoughts reinforce one's creativity, whereas, vicious ones cause and augment it's destability.

Destabilised and uncreative mind loses it's peace.
Over a protracted period of time, man's innovation, imagination and reasoning powers cease.

In a saint's mind, no thought can cause any disturbance and therefore, in hard times, calmness, serenity and peace of mind in him remains in abundance.

By meditation, we could unravel and alter latent frequency bands of both heart and mind.
Ways and means to stamp out diseases and control of natural disasters we may find.

Meditation, certainly, improves concentration of thought-train.
Thus, hitherto unknown faculties, one could, at will, tame.

Positive and unselfish thoughts energise both body and soul.
Whereas, negative selfish ones, moribunds one's conscience and thus take a heavy toll.

Positivity and altruism occurs with due practice in the face of discomfort and many a odd.
Help us in successfully training our minds, Oh our Lord !

BUSINESS MANAGEMENT

If be all and end all of your business is just making money,
It would, then, be futile to expect every day in your

business absolutely bright and sunny.

To be successful, make yourself such a credible force in the eyes of 'one-n-all' that everyone swears by you.

Put relentless and sincere efforts to ensure that everyone has implicit faith and unshakable trust in you.

Don't let anyone have a chance to point a finger at your character, scruples, behaviour, ethics and morals.

And don't ever make the mistake of living on your past laurels.

Those, who, through their business cheat others in order to make quick buck,

obviously forget that, at the end of their meaningless strife, their final spiritual score would be just sweet & blissful duck.

It doesn't matter if you, as a business man, make lesser profit in comparison as long as you keep your self-respect, inner peace and rhythm in-tact.

Be innovative, have technological edge, work ethically with a global vision and remain steadfast throughout as a matter of fact.

Think miles ahead like a champion does in a game of chess.

And, don't ever allow your faculties be impaired under any duress.

Sharpen your mind to have extended wit, wisdom and vision

When, confused, communicate with your inner conscience in silence and solitude and seek His decision.

Learn to encourage your work-force and tap their full-potential.
Remember sharing of your profits graciously and magnanimously with them is more than essential.

Your graceful gentlemanly conduct would make you besides a successful businessman, a darling of 'one-n-all'. Remember, after you're gone, rather than your accumulated wealth & properties out of your business, only your ethics & morals if any, people would very fondly & respectfully, recall !

SILENCE AND SOLITUDE

It helps one talk to Him and Have His company.
It helps one coordinate all His frequencies and
create a melodious symphony.

In it, one can easily dive deep within and
find out the cause and location of impurity and dirt.
After identification, remedial measures can be
taken so that it may no longer cause disorder and hurt.

With it, one comes back to mother earth.
Believe me, with sincere practice, you'll realise even amidst
all noises and company, silence and solitude isn't in dearth.

It helps one feel one's own pulse and fathom
it's true strength.
Soon, one starts perceiving this otherwise,
unfathomable inner world's breadth and length.

In the initial stages of spiritual ascendancy, It's a must.
Like, before tempering of Iron, one has to remove it's rust.

It helps stabilize one's mind
by knocking off anger, passion, greed and helps turn one,
serene and sublime.
It's pure Gold.
With it's use, one can get self under a complete hold.

It's important for any worthwhile
spiritual communication.
Remember, for it, one doesn't have to give anyone a
justification.

One can get it without singing a rhyme.
Therefore, how about initiating yourself
into it, without losing any more time !

BOSS MANAGEMENT

Remember, no one is without a boss
and, his management could save you from avoidable loss.

Be aware what does he expect
and know well what does he respect.

Get interested in what he has interest.
Keep him humoured with your wit and jest.

Never speak ill of him especially at his back.
Remember, if you do, it's a sure way to get a 'sack'.

Deal with his better-half with reverance and tact.
Remember, you're dealing with boss's boss, as a matter of
fact.

Keep him posted with what you're doing and what do you
have in mind.

and don't leave at the end of the day, job or work entrusted behind.

Be loyal and honest about your job
and always and every time make him feel that he is the boss.

Praise him when due and voluntarily help him when, for him, chips are down.
Do care for his family when he's out of town.

Prove sense of commitment, involvement and devotion,
and help him confine his thoughts on macro aspects in motion.

Do share your happiness and his suffocation, stress and pain.
Don't ever stab at his back for your personal gain.

Remember, you serve at his pleasure
and therefore, make sure in your company he feels relaxed and has time for his leisure.

Don't try and prove him wrong.
Otherwise, he won't let you be there for long.
Give your expert advice and suggestion when asked without inhibition.
But, once clear directions are given, execute with sense of professionalism and astute precision.
Work relentlessly and conscientiously in order to win his confidence, faith and trust
As for real rapport, mutual implicit understanding is a must.
Be pleasant, well-mannered and use common-sense more so in his presence.

Remember, in effective boss management lies your success in essence !

HEALTH MANAGEMENT

Whenever you make your body a garbage bin,
rest assured, you're committing against yourself a great sin.
Learn to make it a habit to inhale deep breaths at all times.
And, don't you ever put yourself under stress and duress because of 'dimes'.

With, each breath, learn to pronounce with reverance your God's name without moving tongue and lips
And, don't you ever remain engrossed day in and out in only collecting 'chips'.

Engage yourself in such thoughts and actions that are going to make you feel proud.
And, learn to say a stern 'No' to yourself for fast foods, drinks, tobacco, alcohol and drugs without any hesitation or a doubt.

Follow the maxim of 'eat to live' and Not 'live to eat'.
And, try to find vegetarian substitutes to egg, white and red meat.

Let virtues of self control and temperance guide you when it comes to quantity for intake.
And don't mix up water along with your food for God's sake.

Relish by chewing well in your mouth every bit of your food.
And, while having it, remain calm, serene and in a joyful mood.

In every meal, have only so much that thereafter, you feel good and light.
Remember, what to have and in what quality and quantity is only your birth-right.

Do find out adequate time over each day to burn your fat through Yoga and exercise.
and about disciplining your body, remain steadfastly firm and precise.
Looking after health is an everyday affair.
Remember, sufferings due to your ill-health, none with you can or going to share.

Big hulk and big muscles do not necessarily mean a great health.
The barometer is the nimbleness, agility, inner strength, happiness, body resistance and stealth.

Consider every moment in your life as His personal benign gift
and keep absorbed in activities which provide your psyche the requisite lift.

Make it a habit to have a cheerful disposition throughout the day.
And, keep your ego, anger, greed and lust at bay.

Make efforts to breathe pure air, consume plenty of pure water and choose only vegetarian food.
And, don't allow materialistic forces of this world overtake your pristine and ever happy mood.

God has given you so graciously a near perfect body.
Therefore, in nurturing and looking after it, it's more than

unfair to be shoddy.

Remember, if you care for your body, mind and soul right from an early age.

All the cosmic energies would remain enshrined in your body cage.

You would then be competent enough to decide for yourself when to call it a day

and while living, have a mesmerising halo around with many a cosmic ray.

LEADERSHIP

It needs to be attempted with visible initiative, enthusiasm and vigour.

Spirit of self-sacrifice for nourishment of moral values, in a leader, is the only trigger.

To be effective, he must determine what is reality

and then ponder about proper and appropriate actions and then act with unflinching resolve with faith in self and Him in totality.

Fearless calmness in crisis and quick decision in action are the two hallmarks of a good leader.

Ability to concentrate like that of a vivacious reader.

Leadership is a trust that must be upheld first and foremost at all times.

To lead only by virtue of inheritance in modern times is expecting sweetness out of limes.

It's knowledge, maturity and spiritual strength in application, the rarest privilege when enjoyed with dignity and the resultant honour provides supreme elation.

The led see in their leader, their God in action.
Leader must therefore look at their led as if his own extension.

Mutual respect, faith, trust and confidence converts the team into an ideal sample.
Remember, in the realm of leadership, there's nothing more infectious than personal example.

Leadership isn't a matter of hunch or native ability.
It can be analysed, organized systematically and learnt by most individuals with ordinary capability.

Leader must exhibit visible signs of spiritual grace.
The idea of tackling the root cause of problem rather than symptoms, he must embrace.

It doesn't come about by birth but by consistent sincere efforts and many a try.
In learning from other's mistakes, key to successful leadership undoubtedly lie !

TAKE A STEP

A time comes in everyone's life
when, one is required to take hard decision.
One has to address oneself then,
concentratedly to the problem and
fathom pros and cons with precision.

As both horizontals and verticals make
the picture complete,

One needs courage to venture out
when darkness of night is dense and deep.

Many people's experience suggest that
those who, take the first step.
generally never repent.
Come out of thousands of mallet
strokes without a dent.

Pre-requisite to success is to have a clear vision.
Take help of your inner strength for
that vital decision.

Having done that, one has to set
a practical goal.
Thereafter, in the pursuit
of it's achievement, put one's heart and soul.

All difficulties and problems enroute,
have their own cure.
Dedication, sincerity and devotion to
the cause, for any meaningful
success, have to be there for sure.

Some moments in life pose a
great challenge.
Epitome of maturity and confidence
lies in accepting them with a smile
without losing balance.

Remember, life isn't a bed of roses.
One who remains indecisive
or doesn't take timely decision, finally loses.

CHILD MANAGEMENT

If a child lives with hostility,
he learns to fight.
If a child lives with respect,
he learns to respect other's right.

If a child lives with ridicule,
he learns to be shy.
If a child lives amidst love and affections,
he generally turns out to be a good 'guy'.

If a child lives with shame,
he learns to be guilty and hurt.
If a child lives with acceptance and friendship,
he learns to find love with the world.

If a child lives with security,
he learns to have faith and trust.
If a child lives with fairness,
he learns to be honest and just.

If a child lives with approval,
he learns to love only self.

If a child lives with charity,
he learns to help.

If a child lives with encouragement,
he learns to explore his abilities to create,
If a child lives with praise,
he learns to appreciate.

If a child lives with criticism,
he learns condemnation,

If a child lives with fear,
he learns to be gutless and without positive imagination.

Parents, teachers & the society collectively has a great responsibility in shaping the future of our next generation. Their efforts could alone ensure either upliftment or degeneration.
Indeed as parents, you could make or mar your child
by converting him into either a useful citizen or a wanton wild.

LIFE JOURNEY MANAGEMENT

My bags are packed and I'm about to go
at the end of my life-long show.

I know I should travel light if it's a must,
not withstanding, I've to now carry tons of loads on me, I trust.

Some bags are full of lies and some with deceit,
some with worldly lusts and some with soiled linen and sheet.

To top it all, despite my riches, my pockets are more than bare.
Despite so many domestic helpers, relatives and friends,
no one is ready to go along and take my care.

I'd be gone soon with the gust of breeze
just like in autumn, leaves drift off the mother-trees.

From great heights, I'd then, like a leaf, embrace mother earth.
Leaving all my collections and fortunes behind which, I had

been piling up soon after my birth.

How I wish I'd known that spiritual possessions are lighter than even the thin air,
Whereas, the rest is like a big snare.

Having seen the number, size and awkwardness of these loads, I'm getting cold feet.
With low and dim spirits, I now await to set off on a hitherto unknown beat.

How I wish I'd known it would end so soon !
I would have definitely done something meaningful in order to be at the end of this journey, cool, calm, composed and serenely brilliant like the full moon.

PERCEPTIONS MANAGEMENT

Quality of our lives, to a great extent, depends on our perceptions.
Negativity of our mind induces misunderstandings and misconceptions.

First and foremost, we must know that, if, we want others to be happy, We have to practice compassion.
And, if we want to be happy, we have to again practice compassion.

As a matter of fact, if we perceive everyday as the first day of rest of our life.
Then, it would just be a cake-walk without any sufferings, privations and strife.

Our perceptions must let passion replace our fear.
Instead of boundaries, we must let new horizons look near.

We must perceive this world in a manner that, to us, it matters less, and, our inner voice more,
in order to sort our a problem, as a matter of perception, we must hit at it's very core.

We must perceive a dead end to be a good place to turn around.
For success in life, our perceptions of facts must lead us to decisions, both timely and sound.

Perceptions-wise, we should be clear that no matter how big or soft or warm our bed is, we still have to get out of it.
And, throughout our lives avoidable worries and tensions consume our energies endlessly and mercilessly bit by bit.

Remember, the glass is half empty, or half full is only a matter of one's perception.
Brain is like a parachute, it functions only when it's open without any exception.

Therefore, in order to perceive situations correctly and accurately, we have to get rid of all mental blocks.
Otherwise, it would be analogous to finding amongst cloth pieces a black cloth piece in pitch dark night in a big box.

LIFE SIZE CHALLENGE MANAGEMENT

I find everyone unusually busy in worldly chores like a honey bee.
As if, in this world, for the locks holding all the happiness, money is the only key.

People all over the world, are generally so busy that they have no time even to notice wrinkles on their face.

Their time speeds past as distances in a world class car-race.

Then, all of a sudden, near one's end, everyone gets confronted with a hard and rude impending shock.
His past and the way he went about wasting his life, then, only mock.

Body gets cared with food, water, air and rest but no one thinks about the soul.
Poor thing remains unnourished and uncared for like burnt out coal.

Nourishment and enrichment to soul is only, through spiritual food.
A genuine teacher can alone guide and get one in right frame of mind and mood.

Without soul's upliftment by each day, one's worldly growth would be as if, without any balance.
This is exactly what one has to accept in life as the greatest challenge.

Therefore, realisation of hard facts of life at an early age are more than vital.
Only materialistic growth without spiritual ascendancy is just suicidal.

BREATH MANAGEMENT

If you think of Him and mutely call His name by each deep breath,
Nothing would ever scare you not even your death.
Your thinking horizons would completely change.

And then nothing would ever appear strange.

Hither to unknown, most compassionate and soothing words from your tongue would just flow out.
And nothing would ever put you in a doubt.

Your eyes would perceive truth and positivity anywhere
And then, nothing would ever appear to be unfair.

Your mental prowess would remain engaged in only doing good to all,
Nothing would ever disturb your inner rhythm and draw you in a brawl.

Your face would always radiate His own cosmic light,
Nothing would ever deter you from doing just right
Your gaze would humble and sublime anyone,
nothing would ever mar your spiritual progress, pleasure and fun.

Your body would remain charged with a great magnetic attraction,
Nothing would ever cause any worry or mental affliction.

Doing and achieving it, is a matter of one honest try.
That's the only way to end once for all this world's hue and cry !

SEX MANAGEMENT

Swami Vivekananda said, "Semon is God in motion",
The same flows out after fulfilment of sexual indulgence in a fit of deep desire and emotion.
The drive and desire for the opposite sex is more than

natural.

Infact, it's absence is more than unnatural.

Two essentials must be met before, with someone, you share your body.

Without mutual love and reverence, play is bound to be shoddy.

Sharing bed with someone is a business rather serious

Forcing someone, on to it, is rather perilous

Size of male's organ is perhaps not as significant as the size and quality of his head and heart.

Holding your partner in arms passionately before, during and after one is done, is, the game's vital part.

Foreplay is most significant perhaps, as much as the actual act.

Sincere, subtle flattery and appreciation before and after reinforces mutual satisfaction as a matter of fact.

Some hurry up as if, in a mad rush.

Then, while the partner demands, they bury their head breathing heavily as if, in slush.

Some think once they're done, they've achieved 'Action total'.

And, get off like after paying up bills, one leaves the hotel.

If your bed-mate hasn't looked satisfied at the end of it,

It would be apt if you're called a nit-wit.

Remember, clean bodies in clean environment and with clean hearts have a better chance to make it a memorable experience and a grand success,

whereas, deceitful hearts with guilt inherent in the act

would invariably land up both in a veritable mess.

Sexual desire, play and indulgence is a significant part in anyone's life.

Since it's an art and art comes through practice and therefore to be gorgeously wonderful in it, one has to sincerely strife.

LIFE MANAGEMENT

Like after a successful event, the event manager gets pats from 'one n all'.

Similarly after a meaningful and purposeful life,

one deserves bouquets from all and sundry no matter life span was long or short.

To manage the story, bring in it realism, purpose and sincerity.

And then go ahead writing your life story with indelible ink of selfless actions with dedication and clarity.

The practice of life management isn't just to make only living but to make the soul grow.

In the game of Basket-ball, remember, in order to score one has to eventually dispossess the ball and throw.

These days, Greed of being somebody and fear of being nobody is driving people mad.

Obviously these people have lost the discretionary power to know what's good for them & what's bad.

Don't let the dissatisfaction of yesterday distaste your today resulting in distrust for your tomorrow.

Just enjoy what you are deep inside and don't let any negative thought enter your head which leads you to despair and sorrow.

You are required only to manage your present giving top most priority to your inner voice.
That's the best way to get His personal benign gifts as per your desire and choice.

This body is His personal gracious gift to you and therefore, you ought to take its care the way you do to people given gifts in life.
This ethos when put to practice, will ensure that you have pain-free and stress-free life.

If and when you lead a truthful life, there is nothing to fear and worry about
The Almighty and omnipresent would personally protect and care for you without an aota of doubt.

❏

4

MANAGEMENT
IN THE CONTEXT
OF OUR
'GLOBAL VILLAGE'

THE RELIGIOUS IMBROGLIO

Body is your temple and God somewhere within,
Whereas, in the name of God and religion you perpetuate only sin.

Don't think when you kill hapless and mute in the name of Your God, you'll be destined to heaven.
You're bound to get hell as deserves any demon.

It belies my imagination, how you get convinced that your God will be pleased if, you kill others,
You'll surely get His wrath for orphaning innocent children and widowing mothers.

All religions preach love of mankind,
whereas you, in the name of religion, become a savage beast devoid of civilized mind.

If you keep your religion confined within you and be with Him at all times
you will be revered like a monumental sacred shrine.

You've no right to take others life on any pretext
and don't bring in religion and stir up emotions under your and other's chest.

Loving Him and His creation is the only sacred duty.
It is selfless love which can make you understand the real definition of beauty.

You all acknowledge that Ishwar, Allah, Christ and Guru Nanak are all manifestations of one God.

Since all have preached universal love and brotherhood, rule of love and not by a iron rod.

Interpretations of our religions are more than absurd and suit our convenience.

We sacrilege our respective faith and take undue advantage of our God's benevolence and lenience.

We have no right to preach what we don't understand. Major issues we merrily forget, but, upon unimportant ones, for vested gains, must we take war like stand ?

By following any religion in true letter and spirit, one can do only good to humanity, regardless of caste and creed.
Remember, He will wield His stick for your each wrong deed.

Any religion is pure love, kindness and goodness without personal selfish thought.
Management of entire life based on these tenets alone, could, save the entire humanity from a stinking rot !

A SUBJECT MOST MISUNDERSTOOD

East and West are the two great supplements.
Achievements of both to collective humanity are great compliments.

One stands for spiritual growth and the other, for materialism.
Undoubtedly, a judicious mix of both can give rise to balanced humanism.

Like a pauper can't help another pauper,
a bottle can't hold anything in it without a proper stopper.

A rich man alone, can help those, who need his help
Spiritual strength alone, would help him utilize for a good

cause, his wealth.

Being rich and being in a position to help the needy is materialism.

Inner urge to help the 'Have Not's and suffering humanity is spiritualism.

Therefore, both are a must.
Balanced rhythm and genuine quest for both is rather just.

Those, who profess that materialism and spiritualism are poles apart,
obviously don't understand the inter-relation of a horse and cart.

I feel both East and West have to, from each other, learn a lot.
In order to establish a very healthy and cordial relationship between the "Haves" and "Have Not".

Take the example of Mrs. Anita Roddick; a millionairess who, denotes today, a perfect synthesis of East and West,
That's why, she possesses worldly riches alongwith inner peace and rest.

Why can't we all practice the same ?
Learn from each other without any complex or shame !

OUR PLANET TURNS INTO PARADISE

No one remembers Him when the going is good,
whereas, everyone should.

Everyone remembers only Him when the spirits are dim.
It just shows how selfish we are right upto our brim.

Remember Him and sing Thy praises since in Him alone,
the ultimate truth lies.
He alone could show all the way to paradise.

We're all His spark.
Alas ! we keep groping in dark.

Aimlessly we wander and seek physical pleasure.
Don't bother to fathom the inner voice by any measure.

Since, we keep loving ourselves and not His creation,
the end result is enormous misery and frustration.

The panacea of all ills lies in selfless love
like, that of a mother.
The pleasure and solace that one derives out of it
lies in no other.

Love is the language of soul.
It encompasses humane, kind and benevolent actions
for His creation as a whole.

It's the key to salvation.
The only way for anyone's immortalisation.

The true practice of this magical
four letter word 'love', could only save this planet.
Since, all religions of world have this as their basic tenet.

He is with you with His limitless love at all times.
Why don't you shun hatred, jealousy, anger, pride
and ego and help make our planet devoid of all crimes ?

Sooner you realize, better it is.
That's the only way to reinforce and spread His gracious
bliss !

PRESERVATION OF HUMANITY

Slender is the thread between sanity and insanity,
both are immensely innate in all humanity.

There are some who, understand what their conscience
dictates and act in time.
There are others who, defy inner voice and bend towards
crime.

One who listens, may outwardly suffer, but possesses inner
peace and real pleasures.
The other remains spiritually bankrupt, although amidst
abundant worldly treasures.

Some plants give fragrant flowers even amidst scum and
dirt
Where as, some, even amidst expert hands, look unhealthy
and hurt.

Experience of all man-kind abundantly proves that love is
epitome of all civility.

It generates fellow feelings of respect for all and virtue of
humility.
Without which, life seems monotonous and dull
like, a rust-eaten ship-hull.

No one, except oneself, can help in this respect anyone
Otherwise, the whole life becomes like that of a
disillusioned nun.

Genuine and selfless love alone, is panacea for all ills,
plaguing our world today.
Otherwise undoubtedly all of us, one day, through our
nose, would pay !

EAST OR WEST EVERYTHING IS JUST THE SAME

Dialogues differ but life stories generally are same.
Hearts are identical all over the world despite a variety of name.

Reactions of men and women to mundane actions are so akin regardless of place.
Situations themselves are so similar in this life's race.

For example, infants all over cry the same way.
Rooster welcomes sun rise everywhere each day.

Owls and dogs provide ample warning as soon as they perceive Death God in near vicinity.
Deers and rabbits exhibit anywhere the same impulse of timidity.

Cobra hoods up to attack.
For short-sightedness and inefficiency, all over, managers get a sack.

Mothers force nipple into crying baby's lips.
Shopkeepers and businessmen before closing for the day, in uniquely similar manner, count their chips.

Tethered calf runs towards mother cow and affords her while sucking, both pleasure and pain.
Ground oozes out same musky smell after a few drops of rain.

Young maids feel shy and blush in awkward situations irrespective of caste and creed.
Instinct of self preservation is predominant everywhere

regardless of breed.

All, are in fact, acting for pre-set and pre-determined time span.

Let us realise this reality and foster love regardless of artificial boundaries between man and man.

NEW HORIZONS

In our mountains, there's always yet another hill.
Somewhere, on this beautiful earth of ours,
a terrorist awaits for another kill.

In our deserts, there's always yet another dune.
Somewhere, on this lovely earth of ours,
someone is misusing His blessings and boon.
In our sky, there is always yet another star.
Somewhere, on this fascinating earth of ours, an addict
is searching yet another drug joint and a bar.

Over our seas, there's always yet another tide.
Somewhere, on this magnificent earth of ours,
someone's sister or daughter is being
compelled to commit suicide.
In our pastures, there's always yet
another green grass blade.
Somewhere, on this fantastic earth of ours,
a sex-maniac is planning to rape a
young maid.

In our fertile minds, there's always yet another thought.
Somewhere, on this charming world of ours,
someone is laughing at someone else's cost.

In our oceans, there's always yet another
under current.
somewhere, on this marvellous world of ours,
dead body of a hapless and innocent is
being secretly burnt.

In the field of weaponary, there's always yet
another gun.
Somewhere, on this enchanting world of ours,
a mother sheds silent tears on barbaric
and cold blooded murder of her innocent son.

In our metropolitan cities, there's always yet another lane.
Somewhere, on magically alluring world of ours,
someone steals and murders another
for want of a grain.

Amidst Valleys and Mountains, there's always
yet another picturesque sight.
Somewhere, on this attractive world of ours,
someone is being choked since, he dared
to clamour for his and other's basic birth right.

In encatchment areas, there is always yet
another brook.
Somewhere, on this superb earth of ours,
someone is devising new ways
and means to cheat and crook.

If somehow, these negative forces on our
beautiful earth of ours, go underground,
There would be real peace, happiness and
prosperity all around. !

ONE HUMANITY, ONE EARTH

East or West, North or South, all places are
after all, on our one earth.
Where, each one of us, has somewhere or the other,
his hearth.

Native place has no doubt, it's own attractions;
where, there is a deep sense of belonging and
spontaneous natural affectionate reactions,
and where, having come back, one finds not much has
changed.

Yet, there are some places on the same earth, where
environments make you behave like, most unnatural
as if, deranged.

If, all of us adopt our beautiful planet and
call it our native place,
the attitude itself, could be instrumental in getting
some solace.

All of us have to have, feelings for the
oppressed, whereever they be.
because for the concept of universal brotherhood,
it alone, has the key.

I wonder, why don't we all stir up when natural
calamities like volcanoes, typhoons, quakes,
famine & epidemics take a heavy toll of our brothers
and sisters any where on our planet !
Why don't we all have, to govern our affairs, one humane
senate ?

It's high time world over, towards this end, all of us

should show our collective will and inclination.
Without which, as time goes by, our narrow and parochial
vested interests would keep on reinforcing our hesitation.

The ethos of genuinely caring for one another, regardless
of man-made barriers, has to be fundamentally the bottom
line.
Otherwise, hypocricy and affectation would only
add to suffering for all of us and manifest into a really
bad time !

PROSPERITY OR ANNIHILATION

Like all have limits of patience, so has our mother nature.
In the light of this fact that man is only a miniscule part of
nature and not it's master, he must understand his overall
stature.

Scientific advancement of man has caused so far
enormous pollution to land, water and air.
All over our globe, he'd been effecting it without any care.

That's how, dumps of toxic wastes on land, water and
pollutants in air, have caused deaths and sufferings hither
to unknown.

That's exactly why, humans all over the world are seething
out with excruciating pain and bursting out with deafening
moan and groan.

If pollution goes on unabated at the present rate.
Life in present forms on our earth would soon become a
subject of a vintage.

Living on polluted land, drinking of polluted water and

breathing toxic gases have to have a debilitating effect on the purity of our hearts and mind.

That's why there is so much of social sufferings and our actions; most dishonest, deceitful and unkind.

Felling of trees, untreated industrial wastes, nuclear-waste, toxic pollutant's are taking a heavy toll of human life and degrading it's quality regardless of man-made barriers.

The affected land, water and air have become universally deadly viruses carriers.

If we, as intelligent humans, now, don't pay heed to this prime need of the hour,

for all of us and for our young generations, despite scientific progress, real grapes would remain sour.

Green revolution all over the world can help save this otherwise sinking ship.

Strict universal adherence to rules and regulations for emissions and disposal of toxic water is as important as the electronic chip.

Remember, we can't survive withoutl our benign mother nature, whereas she can.

Therefore, fooling around with it anymore is an unpardonable crime against self as well as against many a innocent hapless man.

Time is fast running out.

Let us therefore, without any inhibitions, work towards saving our planet without any apprehensions or doubt.

Also, let us develop ourselves in complete harmony with nature,

and then, enhance amongst countless galaxies, collective
human race's celestial powers and stature !

SILVER LINING

Times are blissfully changing for better.
Realisation of respect for human beings, their
rights, dignity and thoughts is the crux of the matter.

Bitter enemies of past have now a fair
chance to shake hands.
There seems now, a viable possibility of
having one humane world government for all lands.

We've to collectively think ways and
means to stop Acid-rain.
Provide one 'n' all a shelter, clothes and adequate grain.

We've to ensure that Green-house
effect doesn't become a reality.
Spectrum and quality of life, for all on the globe,
has to be collectively reviewed by all scientists,
engineers and doctors in it's totality.

We've to ensure that meteoroids and asteroides
from outer space don't collide
with our earth and cause thousands
of N Bombs worth a bang.
For that, all our astroscientists and space scientists
have to put their heads together as members of one gang.

Hand in hand, we've to fight all kinds of viruses and
disease.
Like, as batsmen in test matches, we've to ensure that we

remain on the crease.

Our young generation could then, blossom
in complete freedom without any fears.
Instead of tears and cries then, there would be
only laughters and cheers.

Obnoxious looking war tools and implements
could be used collectively for the good of human race,
blissful peace then, could reign on both our
planet and space.

We could easily channelise all our energies
for peace, preservation and prosperity of all man kind.
Forget our bitter past history and leave it far behind.

Life in the lap of bountiful nature with all
our materialistic and spiritual advancements,
would be a real fun.
One earth, one moon, one human race without
any colour, religion, caste and creed and nationality
under one great Sun !

If we preserve our nature and it's resources are
shared by all,
We won't have 'Haves' and 'Have Nots' and thus,
everyone on the face of our earth, will have
a royal ball.

It's very much possible if, all of us take
bold initiatives and
collective steps in right earnest.
All of us, have to, for attainment of this noble goal,
turn absolutely honest.

HUMAN POWERS

Like nuclear energy isn't bad.
Bad is however, it's misuse.
Human body is a perfect and
flawless God's creation, provided it's not put to abuse.

Powers of this wonderful machines are beyond any stretch of imagination.
All depends on it's balance, health, inner hygiene and sanitation.

Inner vision can travel along sunrays and see what sun can,
concentrated beams of the inner conscience of real saints in a split second, would alter regardless of distance, mental frame of any man.

Human ears can hear voices spoken millions of years ago, the metaphysical form anywhere in this universe at multiple of light's speed, at will, can go.

Mere wish can change orbiting of planets, satellites and stars.
One can free oneself in split second from all kinds of shackles and bars.

Energy enshrined, in a non-living element's atom is so big, vast and massive.
Surely, the same in our (living being's) conciousness would be unimaginably over-powering, over bearing and suppressive !

Spiritual advancement will make one unravel nature's as well as cosmic laws and rules.

One could tour galaxies at will with acquired spiritual knowledge tools.

This virgin field, man needs to fathom and explore,
in order to experience dimensionless pleasures by their core.
In spiritual ascendancy alone, lies the keys.
That is in case, a super human, you ever wish to be !

LIFE ON EARTH AT RAZOR'S EDGE

Man is a contagious disease and with him as a race,
the planet of earth is already sick.
If he doesn't mend his ways soon, like Dinassaurs, his own existence would get a kick.

Our planet, in the present degraded
eco system, can only support five billion.
whereas we're already six and half and keep adding
every year about multiple of ten million.

Let us all understand clearly one important aspect;
Life can coexist only in a balanced natural system as a matter of fact.

Whenever you tamper with nature, things are bound to go wrong.
Enough has already happened and therefore,
let us not impoverish our children's life just for a song !

There is no alternative but to make concentrated effort by all, to keep her green.
That's the only way to make life peaceful, healthy and pristine !

Those who oppose this for vested interests are traitors of mankind.
How long we would continue to be, towards the dire need of our mother-planet, deaf and blind !

THE ECO FACTOR

We all, regardless of caste and creed, ceaselessly breathe the same air.
Sight of our common skies and stars regardless of national boundaries, share.

Alas ! about the purity of our soil, water and air we don't seem to care.
Enormous destruction, collectively we've already caused, yet, we don't seem to be aware.

Sight of chimneys coughing smoke and factory wastes and pollutants don't raise eye-brows and hair.
At this rate, perhaps our beautiful planet would become like Mars ; barren and bare.
Thus, we certainly aren't being towards our future generation, fair.

Breathing pollution-free air and drinking pure water is anyone's pristine birth-right.
We, obviously, seem to have had thick veils all this time obscuring our sight.

Like for tomorrows comforts, one has to prepare today regardless of the calendar date.
Similarly, we have to take stock of stumbling edifice lest we all get too late !

May be, our concerted effort all over the world, would be instrumental in uniting us all,
into one common wealth of all white and black, rich and poor and big and small.

All dedicated towards preservation of ecological balance and pollution-free globe.
The fact that man knows where does his genuine interests lie, sustains my hope.

Towards this end, let us have stringent and applicable to all, global laws and rules
and make subject of preservation of eco-balance, a mandatory part of curriculum at appropriate level in all schools !

CAN ANY ONE TELL ME ?

Honey bees go on collecting
nectar from a common flower,
without a fight.
Man goes on disturbing own
and other's peace day and night.
I don't know why !
Parrots, after days hard labour,
get back home together, chirping merrily all the way.
If man could help it; after
dividing land and sky he would
even divide benign Sun's ray.
I don't know why !
Birds, generally respect their
elders and follow them in perfect formation.

Some men, because of their skin colour,
race or riches call themselves a superior creation.
I don't know why !
Ants perform their duty most
sincerely and run up in a straight line, following a
beaten track.
For selfish petty ends, even
civilised men's personal defences crack.
I don't know why !
Animals drink water from a
common source without a brawl.
Men, states and countries over the
same issue, pounce at each other's throat and prawl
I don't know why !
Trees grow in nearness, hugging and
kissing each other's leaves in
perfect neighbourhood.
Man, only knows how to sermonise and preach
Universal brotherhood.
I don't know why !
Love birds are most sincere to each other and
die in separation.
Both Men and Women through illicit sex, seek
thrill and elation.
I don't know why !

LOUD NOISES OF STILL SILENCE

Fixed gaze of a Mother who has lost her son,
has deafening sounds;
worst than that one hears at the

dead of night from jackals and hounds.
Young widow's face in sad silence,
produces such booms;
worst than that created by thousands of power looms.
Morose and tragedy-struck face of a
lad who's been orphaned, gives
enormous deafening shriek;
like, wailing and crying sounds of sea
birds and animals in crude oil filled creek.
Sad and hunger stuck lifeless eyes of
malnutritioned child, produce
awfully jarring note;
like, in a cemetry, in pitch dark
night, an owl's hoot.
A helpless innocent's mute face has stunning sound;
like that of a thunder-clap
right next to the ears.
I don't know why people's ears
shy away from latent
decibles of innocent's tears.
If, all of us recognise and respect
sounds of sad and grim silence,
we could perhaps, live with that
requisite temperance and balance !

BIGGEST HUMAN FAILING

Some burn & some bury their dead.
While living, on such meaningless
rituals, they lose their head.

Some have their national flag in
white & some in red.
Killing others across man-made
dividing line, is our national
duty they said.

When will we understand that
one who kills & one who gets
killed are one God's own spark ?
How long will we keep waiting for
skies to fall in order to catch a lark ?

Other heavenly bodies don't seem to have any life
whereas our planet has and looks so marvellous
from just outer space.
What a pity ; on the same planet,
human beings have hypocrisy
savagery & treachery as their life's base !

we don't realise that these very
bacteria have wiped out, in
our past, race after race.
Nothing has changed in reality except,
guns & lethal weapons have
replaced good old lance & mace.

It's high time, all of us; big or small, rich or poor
bring about a radical change in our very outlook.
we've to put into practice, without any coloured
interpretations, whats given in our respective most sacred
book.

WHAT A PITY !

These birds are more sensible as,
they don't divide their environment
for a particular breed.

These flowers are far more civilised
as they offer fragrance and aroma
irrespective of our caste and creed.
Fish is free of any artificial barriers.
Honey bees kiss and love all kinds of flowers and for
nectars, become, in return, their pollen carriers.

Sun rays make no distinction.
Monsoon clouds rain without any confined jurisdiction.

Underground creatures share the earth
and live wherever desired without a fight.
Darkness prevails on half of earth at any one time
regardless of national boundaries at night.
Trees don't ever go on strike.
Purify atmosphere for one-'n'-all alike.

Breeze doesn't care about man-made dividing lines.
I don't know why then, man, all over the world,
behaves worse than canines ?

He's been foolish enough to divide land, sky, sea and
on top of all, hearts.
No wonders, he stinks of incivility and rots.

Some propagate even division of outer space,
so that, he may morbid it's tranquillity and sanctity
when, on earth, he's even lost his trace.

His acts make this planet as a whole, stink

like a putrefied garbage bin.
Under some pretext or the other, strangely enough,
he justifies all his sin.

Canines may be very possessive of their territorial rights
but, are at least, loyal.
Their master instead of learning from pets has opted
to be deceitfully selfish and towards
both inner conscience and others, most disloyal.

Only a deadly attack by some organism from outside space
can make him feel the necessity of universal unity.
Otherwise, his religion, national chauvinism, caste, colour
and creed will keep him divided till eternity !

To my mind, he has no options but to mend his ways
otherwise, through his bloody nose, he'ld pay !

COSMIC ATTACK ON OUR EARTH

Fragments of comet lavy hit planet Jupiter and the world
witnessed this hair raising event with awe and fear.
Scars of this impact, her surface, for her life time, is 'gonna'
bear.

What if such a cosmic attack is delivered on our mother-
earth ?
It would aground our dreams and our age-old hearth.

It could trigger massive fires at impact stage,
engulfing flora and fauna in it's fury and rage.

It could shake our earth and bring anything standing
tumbling down.
Coupled with a deafening bang sound.

It could destabilise the whole planet by forcing
her out of the designated cosmic-path.
Well ! in that case, unimaginable destruction is the obvious
after-math.

God is likely to punish all of us by a cosmic attack for our
deeds.
In the guise of various excuses, all of us are sowing such
distructive seeds.

We have no viable defences against such an attack.
He would, in a split second, put earth clock billion years
back.

Therefore, let us not provocate Him anymore and invite
such a punitive reaction !
Instead, let us just keep Him humoured with our righteous
and honest actions !

I'M ALSO A HUMAN BEING

I was born in tatters.
Since then, my body and soul have
been badly battered.
That's why to anyone, whether I live or
die, it doesn't matter.

No one loves me since, I'm born poor.
Whereas, everyone would have,
had I been rich, I'm sure !

I've lived all throughout with that
awful feeling, as if, I're a hunted fugitive.
Just because to anyone, I'd nothing to give.

Abject poverty is the worst curse;
for a poor, in times of need,
there is no one to nurse.

My gnawing hunger and mental distabilised state
drives me to desperation.
I can do any crime in this world
for this wretched stomach, without any hesitation.

This hypocrite society, hates me
when, I perform acts of desperation
to fill my tummy.

For bringing me into this world,
I keep cursing God, my dad and mummy.

I, too, want to lead a life of respect and dignity.
There seems no hope to improve my life's quality.

Sheer helplessness and desperation,
made me do all heinous crimes.

Even, I forgot that self was a
human being at times.

Committing crime and sin, now, have
become my way of life.
Otherwise, how could I had survived ?

Poor children any where in the
world, need love and care.
Otherwise, for sheer survival,
any brutally savage and heinous
crime would they dare !

HYPOCRISY

What's happened to human beings on earth ?
Live throughout with hatred,
greed and anger right from their birth !

Despite civilisation, there is
no let up in human abuse.
People get on to other's throats on any excuse.

Some kill in the name of their prophet,
some for other's money and wallet.

Some for oil.
some for soil.

some for a quick buck,
some for the sake of fun,
exuberance and zest.

worst still is, that killers and terrorrists
lagitimise their dastardly acts
in the name of nationalism and patriotism.
Some attempt to veil these
under disguise of religious
emancipation and chauvinism.

No one seems to think of
mother's, father's, son's, daughter's
brother's and sister's silent tears.
Instead, on mass killings, get
into pseudo national euophoric
moods and celebrate with cheers.

Until one-'n'-all, regardless of
Caste, creed, religion and nationality,

treat others as their own,
people all over this world,
would continue to moan and groan.

How about bestowing upon
everyone here some real sense ?
Otherwise, everyone on this
earth, would, live through
somehow, as absolutely grim and tense !!

EAT TO LIVE

Most people live only to eat.
Everyday, own records of previous consumption they beat.
Net result is, that they get heavier & heavier each day on their feet.
Their accumulated fat & obesity compels them to keep sticking to their seat.

Then, in order to continue to eat,
They run towards health clubs & go on crash diet course.
But, soon enough, they get back to square one as, they don't remove the basic cause or source.

They soon realise the kind of harm they've caused to their body,
& then, eat only easily digestable substitutes or fat-free foods which were earlier considered more than shoddy.
Thus, they reduce their life-span.
Also, no worth while woman looks at them as a man.
Whereas, some people eat only to subsist
& generally hold a healthy and active life in their own fist.

There's no dearth of food on our planet if, all of us become
people of above said second category !
It would help usher in a new chapter in man-kind's history.

Then, no one anywhere, would die of starvation,
nowhere, children would show signs of malnutrition.

Our world society would, at least, get rid of hunger-related
crimes,
all of us thus, would kill two birds with one stone and help
create better times !

WORST CALAMITY OF OUR TIMES

Before you harbour a thought to share your body,
make sure it won't turn out to be shoddy.

An unthoughtful sexual fling
would have that awfully dreadful virus of 'AIDS' on to you
cling.

Then onwards, your life span is anyone's guess.
Also, incredibly a veritable mess.

A sure and painful death thereafter lies in wait.
It's all upto you if you want to have with it a date.

Once you're down with it, for sure your near and dear ones
won't even visit your hospital ward.
Even best paid doctors and nurses, would, find caring for
you rather hard.

As of now, once it's in you, it would cause a sure kill
God alone knows, who would afford for you the doctor's
whooping bill !

This deadly virus would make you hate yourself

You would curse the very thought of having that indwelling deadly demon itself.

Your relatives in order to avoid embarrassment, would avoid even your reference.
You should call it a day as soon as possible would be their latent preference.

While you linger on, no one would like to come anywhere near.
Even on-looker's pities and sympathies you won't get oh dear.

After you're gone, it would be rather tough for anyone to afford you the ceremonious last rites.
Rest assured, no one would like to touch your eye-lids to shut your sights.

Remember, this deadly virus may enter your body though donated blood, saliva, untreated synringe, unprotected sex or indulgence in sodomy.
Once it's homed on, it'd partake only after it has ended your sordid dichotomy.

The unthoughtful pleasure of a few seconds isn't certainly worth it as you ought to brave this ignominious and horrible death.
In order to avoid being prey to it, just think about the aftermath in your weaker moments by each breath.

This virus recognizes no race-colour, caste, creed and man-made barriers.
Just imagine the plight of newly born whose parents are the virus carriers !

Through 'AIDS' nature has found one more way to maintain

ecological balance.

Even when it's cure is found, mother nature, for all your sins, would devise yet another deadlier virus to pose a formidable challenge.

By fooling around, you're only making the Death God's job easy

and also, helping doctors and researchers all over the world to remain busy.

For a care-free life, you've no alternative but to mend your ways.

Otherwise, the way it is spreading all over our globe, whole of humanity is destined to suffer it's wrath by all nights and days.

Seek intellectual and spiritual pleasures rather then moron physical, if at all, seeking only pleasures is your life time goal.

Otherwise, the whole human race should remain prepared for an unprecedented and unimaginable toll !

WORLD PEACE MANAGEMENT

Holy books of all religions and sects are just the same.
Difference however, if any, lies only in the name.

All of these preach universal brotherhood and love for destitutes and 'Have Nots'

Ironically, the ignorant followers have divided the whole humanity in parochial and water-tight sects and lots.

These books are a common and most sacred heritage of the entire human race

But, alas; all the religionists have, since time immemorial, left no stone unturned to sacrilege their respective Holy-book's face.

Holy hymns and scriptures of all religions guide us how to be a useful citizen of this world regardless of caste and creed.
Whereas, their followers had been only
perpetuating and spreading hatred, anger and greed.

Teachings enshrined in all are universal in their applications.
What a pity, so called the most pious ones have gone berserk in their interpretations.

All followers swear by their respective holy book and recite hymns time and again.
Their fanatical perceptions out of what is conveyed alas is the biggest bane.

Peace and real prosperity on our planet lies only in following truthfully what our holy books actually teach.
Let us first practice in our lives their essence before we only preach.

These great holy books of all faiths are a great guide for the entire man-kind.
The most practical way to keep a cool, balanced and healthy mind.

Spiritual emancipation, development and ecstasy hides in correct interpretation and genuine practice of what's written in all holy books.
Otherwise, one can imagine the state of pie made collectively by all sorts of cooks !

❏

5

ANCIENT INDIAN ETHOS OF MANAGEMENT AND ITS ALL TIME RELEVANCE

ANCIENT INDIAN ETHOS OF MANAGEMENT

Science has, no doubt, given us recipes for 'Goodies' of life.

But all the myriads of philosophies and concepts haven't made us feel happy and successful at the end of this life-long strife.

More and More people I come across, I realize they are more dead than alive.

Not realizing that vanities of this world are transient but for amassing worldly wealth some how alone, day in and out, they sweat and strive.

In present, we could act to change and carve out future the way we want.

But, imperfect perceptions of our doctrines, dogmas, rituals and forms have morbid our minds already and continue to haunt.

Our souls all over the world are potentially divine, unfortunately, nobility of thought and unselfish acts are, never in mind.

That's why, insatiable greed for self aggrandisement controls our life span.

We may be successful money making machines but our hearts and minds are worse that the reverse of a frying pan.

Our souls are dead much before our bodies perish

because, thoughts of changing our external environment for self alone, life-long, we cherish.

People argue that, what we are, is, due to our past.
I wonder, how long this past would last !

We should all get absorbed with what we, as a human race, want to be in future.
If we can't comprehend, then, at least let us make the basic elements and concepts of our holy books and scriptures our tutor !

Each one speaks and guides to the Truth ultimate and energises us to go on doing good.
Otherwise, what do you expect from this body which is worse than a dead wood ?

Hatred and jealousy undoubtedly rebounds with compound interest.
Anger, ego and greed then foster and infest.

These, then attack one's conscience and soul.
Nobility of thought, divinity of soul then, take a heavy
toll.

What's left is, only money making machine guided by savage animal instincts.
Then onwards, body even before death, perpetually stinks.
Money-making is important but more important is making unselfish thoughts and words.
Otherwise, what's different between you and that fourlegged animal in herds ?
There is a dire need to manage successfully our internal and external environment for the good of whole man-kind.
Otherwise, we alone, would be responsible for leaving dead earth devoid of any divinity behind.

By combining scientific and technological elements of the West and spiritual values of self-sacrifice and self-control of ancient India, we could produce a prototype far superior than any as yet;

a perfect synthesis of progressive actions with spiritual calmness I bet.

Best of management, and backed by impure conscience, without ethical values, is more than a farce.

Only ethical principles, spiritual and holistic approach to management could, turn it into a real and meaningful prosperity oriented dye-cast.

Today, management needs to be based on two basic truths of life; firstly, the essential infinitude of all souls and the inherent divinity.

Secondly, the essential oneness of universe, life in all forms and the inherent connectivity and solidarity.

While the first one, would make managers realise how potentially divine is their soul

and how can they appreciate the manifestation of that very divinity anywhere and everywhere as a whole.

The second one, would make them unfold how essentially all life is just one,

deeply inter-connected, resting on all pervading consciousness and material wealth-wise, meaningless when all is done.

In the seamless world of today, nations though independent, are indeed getting more and more inter-dependent.

International alliances, international organisations, international laws are the order of the day.

Managers with narrow and myopic visions of only producing "Surplus" somehow, would obviously soon have "No Say".

Remember, the ultimate end of all work is service of mankind.

Divinity in a few, then, serves all in a great divine-bind.

Once the practical aspect of this great ethical value of ancient Indians is understood and put to practice by those in managerial chair,

Everyone would, then, conscientiously work out own responsibilities, cooperate and gladly share.

Plurality is only on the surface and at spiritual core level, all are essentially one.

It is this comprehension which, would make everyone put relentless effort together and in pursuit of excellence, nothing is left undone.

Also remember, different races with their civilisations are manifestation of divinity in variety.

The barometer of their civility however, is measured by how much women, children, destitute and "Have Nots" get respect in that society.

Ethos of presence of divine motherhood in all women is worth recognition.

This ethical value, when practiced by all, would recharge and reenergise His whole creation.

Our forefathers believed that we came from joy, life long

pursue joy and finally dissolve in joy
whereas, life-long pursuit of materialistic joy is, in fact, a decoy.

Inner joy out of self-less service, helps one achieve unalloyed bliss.
Which, should be, the real goal of everyone's life and that, one can't afford to miss.

People are meant to be loved and material things used, but, unfortunately today, what's practiced every where is, other way round.
That's why, basically, complex problems, worries and tensions haunt us and before any meaningful take off, we run aground.

Knowledge of this truth would motivate anyone to only think and act for the good of others.
Then, it, Gyana (Knowledge) would compel each one to treat others regardless of man-made barriers as only blood brothers.

Imagine, the potential of such a cooperative movement of 'one-n-all' backed by pure conscience and divinity of soul !
Scientific and technological tools as servants for the good of the universe as a whole !

This work-culture and ethos would make everyone experience living in the infinite,
using one's known and latent potentialities for a common goal as a birth right.

Remember, bliss is attainable while living in this very world through life of unselfish interests.

Like, pure and potable water is found deep-down after it's been filtered through earth's layers and crests.

Undoubtedly, those who earn wealth only for themselves, sinfully lead this life.
Frustration and failure in the end, makes them repent enormously for this meaningless and wasteful strife.

Like no goading is required for any mother to feed her new born infant.
Similarly, spontaneous "service before self" ethos should be on the minds of all managers and leaders with their actions proving their intent.

Undoubtedly, the root of happiness lies in righteous action.
Legitimately, honest earning should, therefore, be the only attraction.

Root of self control lies in genuine humility,
and one, who has self-control, can inspire the whole world community.

Genuine service of man-kind can only be through knowledge, wisdom and self-realization.
Possession of these attributes in all, would, give rise to a benevolent hitherto, unknown creed and civilisation.

Management is about motivating people to do what you want them to do in a spirit of kith and kin.
The Ancient Indian philosophy of management begins with motivating and equipping both leader and the led in realising the essential divinity and infinite potential in all within.

West places matter over spirit, while Hindus the other way round.

Logically, only after internal excellence, one could seek the same on external ground.

When managers and leaders lead by personal example, collective performance of such managers and the managed in a group is bound to be a rare sample.

Remember, those who make money by sinful means, also, squander it sinfully.

At the time of saying the, final "good bye", they leave everything behind most painfully.

Therefore, accumulated money be treated as a "Trust" in one's hand.

Using it for the hapless, destitute and needy is the only idea noble and grand.

Profit and productivity managers in the industrial world are in great demand.

Achievers of material success at any cost are termed "Go getters" and are considered an exclusive brand.

Their games for profit alone is like playing Tennis with eye on scoreboard and not on the ball.

In the process, altruistic ethics are ignored or kept at last priority-call.

Remember, 'you may fool the whole world down the pathway of life and get pats on your back as you pass.

But, your final reward will be heartaches and tears if you've cheated the man in the glass'.

Today, more and more managers however, are realizing

that, in the ultimate analysis, integrity pays and one doesn't have to cheat to win.
There is no point in committing with each breath sin after sin.

Problems would continue to confront as we deal with both tangible and intangible.
Most are, our own creations as, our perceptions become lopsided, hazy and imperceptible.

When confronted with a tough and knotty one, there is need to take some quiet time to reflect,
seek guidance from divine powers enshrined within, put things into proper perspective and let the problem on it's own deflect.

Self-introspection and success through ethical means is righteous management.
This alone, could foster mutual faith, trust and goodwill between individuals and world society and provide sound basis for positivity and encouragement.

Acting ethically, is the vital responsibility of any leader. Signal out of the post-mortem reports of "big giant's failure that the days of intelligent utilitarian management were over, is quite clear to any analytical reader.

Our forefathers philosophised long time back that work be treated both as a worship and meditation.
This concept in practice today, would, end all demonic miseries and usher ambience of utmost satisfaction.

Not only that, the homogenous and judicial balanced mix of science and this "mind set" towards work would bring

peace, prosperity and happiness to whole world in its wake.
Remember, without spiritual values as the bedrock basis,
corporate philosophies and strategies, no matter how
brilliant, are totally fake.

Companies with ethics, would imbue their work-force with
"do or die" spirits and real motivation.
The led would cheerfully accept formidable challenges and
in top-gear efficiency, seek inner bliss and elation.

West advocates organisational structure and systems to
face challenges ahead.
But, without spiritual values like "Service Before Self"
fairplay, harmony and cooperation, courtesy, humility and
gratitude, organisations would even before launch, be
dead.

Let material success not impede vital spiritual strength
and let spiritual strength of 'One-n-all' cooperatively unfold
peace and progress throughout the continents.

Today, rise in material affluence is at the cost of spiritual
degeneration.
Therefore, the whole world society suffers from the disorder
and violence of misplaced values and judgement and
consequent insinuation.

Pursuit of personal gains, thought about only self and most
selfish nature of each one are then, in global context
massive impediments.
Causing huge barriers in genuine and sincere interactions
all over and polluting global business environment with
unfilterable sediments.

Business, in today's and tomorrow's world, naturally, therefore, must go beyond mere money and bread.
People have to link their present with our Global Village's future instead.

Vision of mankind's collective future, could, let the world society regain much needed balance.
Work places would then become more attractive, effective, productive and life full of verve and buoyance.

Industrially and economically advanced societies are viewed as dangerous wilderness.
Where, misplaced values and disrespect for life has, generally, disenchanted everyone in the absence of gracious benevolence and kindness.

That's why, they, now, seriously try and find solution and look towards the orient East.
Where, even in object poverty, people blissfully live and taste divine spiritual feast.

Contentment, inner calm and happiness are result of our own perceptions.
Meditation, introspection and faith in Him and self would make our minds churn out only noble and righteous thoughts since their inceptions.

Therefore, it is more than important to cleanse our minds with the broom of divine knowledge and wisdom
and carve out first and foremost, within us, a humane, gracious and benign kingdom.

Influence of such a powerful kingdom would humble any and everyone and bring him in it's fold.

Then onwards, a cultural bind of discipline, workolihism, reverence and mutual trust in the group would compel everyone to stay in it's hold.

Any organisational set up would then be tensionless and stress-free.

Men and machines at all levels would blossom in peak efficiency, like various parts of a healthy tree;

Ever ready to brave any tempest, gale or a storm, adjusting to prevalent winds as a self mechanism enshrined in common standard operating procedure or a norm.

These days, most organisations after touching economic heights soon lose sense of purposeness.

Situation is analogous to the plight of a flier whose aircraft, after attaining great heights, becomes rudderless.

When men of a company get a feeling of becoming mere robots or white-collar peons or company live stock, their interaction, both internal and external, are bound to be like the one between stones and a rock.

Such organisations are doomed to fail.

Their robotised and standardised work-force then, fights within and without 'tooth-n-nail'.

That's why, work-force at all levels, in highly advanced and affluent countries are increasingly facing mental troubles and disorder.

Insomnia, stress, heart-attacks, nervous breakdowns, suicides, depressions are accumulatively decaying society's health and order.

West in it's pursuit of modern management culture has all along closed her eyes, towards accompanying "moral horrors" and "spiritual agonies".

East is, also, blindly following the West unmindful of by products, like on narrow mountain track, load-carrying ponies.

Thus, both have focussed their attention and energies today, without any deep thought on our world's tomorrow.

At this rate, the entire mankind is doomed to drown itself in fathomless sea of pain, suffering and sorrow.

Real respect for both work and work-force, is exhibited through altruism, empathy and compassion.

Top efficiency, quality, service, free communications, economic growth flow out of it as a natural outcome without any mental strain and congestion.

Neck breaking new demands due to back-breaking "global competition" is driving the corporate work-force and executives of corporate sector crazy and insane.

To top it all, the top echelons are most selfishly running after personal name, fame or gain.

Here lies the seed of dilution of work-ethos and culture.

The situation is analogous to one carcass amongst many a starved vulture.

Hindus have eulogized a "Yogi" to be a man of culture or a true gentleman.

The corporate world, from top to bottom, needs such "Yogis" who, by their selfless acts would create divine relations between man and man.

Today, if scientific management and technical innovations are providing to have increasing powers to satisfy our materialistic desires in arithmetic progression.

Then, power of desires to have more and more would go on increasing in geometric progression.

Progression in some field and regression in another, by and large, today, are two faces of the same coin.
like, ferocious face and a tame tail are parts of the same lion.

Hindus also believe that, sum total of pleasures and miseries in individual's life and in the whole world are same.
Like, in a ocean, a big wave has rise and fall interconnected through the same transient water-frame.

Success through cheating someone or others, is a delusion.
Tension, fear and loss of mental peace which accompanies exploitation of others make one finally believe that this kind of success is nothing but a colossal illusion.

It's a pity, in our so called civilized world, business thrives today, on innovative means to heist.
People in the system get inextricably involved and are unable to beat a retreat.

A true "Yogi" whose whole life edifice rests on spirituality, sees oneself in others, regardless of race, caste and creed.
Thus, his concentration, energies and faculties get synergised to improve upon self and his entire breed.

Balanced material and spiritual upliftment of all can, alone,

denote progress in real term.
Business activity based on ethics alone, could, supplement these two factors in turn.

Dynamism in business comes with action to overcome weakness and reinforce strength in pursuit of excellence. Without spiritual ethics and genuine love for all, no one can hope to build the requisite temper and resilience.

The ancient Indian ethos of renunciation and 'service before self' is most apt and practical for 'One-n-all' any where.
These two swords in the hands of "Yogi" can knock off evil and take the underprivileged of the world under protective care.

Managers, executives, entrepreneurs and business magnates are all required to be today "Yogis" of such magnitude.
That's how, there can be culture of universal love all over irrespective of longitude and latitude.

Let the management's twin aim universally be material prosperity with spiritual satisfaction.
It would ensure more joyful motivation for work and doing it with perfection, would, hold unique attraction.

A strong will reinforced by renunciation induces divine thought which is the most powerful of all forces. Undoubtedly, a man, in whom, "I, me and my is dead, commands Cosmic powers and possesses world's best pedigreed horses.

Unselfish service not only generates power, it also, brings

out one's best with top efficiency.

The man becomes a world-mover and not only that, induces in others such a divine tendency.

There is an Indian saying "If you serve man today, tomorrow God will serve you".

If this becomes the basic tenet of corporate culture today, tomorrow, a bright future will automatically be reserved for you.

Things would be different even if, ominous beginning in holistic approach to management is started by a minority.

Remember, history is created by the unselfish creative minority and not by the selfish majority.

Besides the recipe for the "Goodies" of life, all of us need the recipe for a good life.

Right now, "goodies"; materialism and good life; spiritualism are separated by a sharp knife.

The knife of misunderstanding, misplaced perceptions and stark ignorance due to which, everyone feels that materialism and spiritualism are poles apart.

While in reality, both are interlinked and interdependent like, the animal and body frame of a horse-cart.

In the glare of technology, we've lost sight of knowledge which, gives us the power of discretion.

From technology, flows out power and all of us are engaged in tasting this only as science's secretion.

Therefore, the consequent growth is lop-sided and a stunted one.

Hence, we need to put into practice a homogenous mix of

philosophies of East and West for the good of mankind in the long run.

Science and technology has made our lives more or less mechanical.

Whereas, human values provide us much needed energy and "go-getter" spirits; so chaste and ethical.

Concept of welfare for self alone is only an extension of "Survival of the Fittest" or Struggle for Existence.

Whereas mutuality, cooperation, love, reverence for all would help achieve highest welfare and a sincere effort would face no resistance.

Amidst cut-throat materialistic competition, only spiritualism can show us the way of peaceful coexistence.

Otherwise, economic wars between races and nations would threaten man's very subsistence.

Our life struggle is dotted with selfishness, avarice and impatience which, cumulatively brings out the worst in us.

Whereas, benign selflessness and healthy cooperation would exhibit the best in us.

Cut throat competition for wealth has given rise to the spirit of money addiction in our younger generation.

In the total absence of ethical values, fear, purposelessness, drug-addiction, neurosis, anxiety, unethical life and untimely death are all signs of degeneration.

Excellence in work according to Indian scriptures, is the highest form of religion.

Also, undoubtedly, nation or race which, refuses to learn

new things is in for a great delusion.

Industry is the manifestation of excellence in man-kind. That's how one can explore and experience the infinite possibilities hidden beneath and leave one's past behind.

Remember, excellence has no end like, there can't be a perfect story.

Meeting of East and West in true spirit would be, in man's history, glorious moments of crowning glory.

Wherever ethics are at work, employees and managers in everlasting relationship are in fray.

Multiangular consensus amongst workers and managers keeps all man made and related problems at bay.

The big question is how does the infinite power within, begin to manifest ?

Indian philosophical scriptures talk about prayer, Yoga, meditation and unselfish acts as ways to harness and utilize the same with the divine zeal and zest.

Prayer makes our individual will coincide with the cosmic will

and when the cosmic will begins to manifest through the individual, he could, at will, infuse life even in still.

When we pray, we are in communion, with the cosmic mind; the mind of our creator.

The worshipping spirit is the most powerful form of energy from which, on other form of energy is greater.

Remember, in companies, where managers and workers pray together,

those companies through thick and thin, stay together.

Then comes Yoga, the path of concentration and meditation.
Through mystic process of breathing, one stirs up infinite power at the base of spinal column and then unites self with the infinite self without any hesitation.

Meditation energises brain's right half ; the divine, creative, potential seat.
Which, in turn, revitalizes and reinvigorates body vibrations, radiance and heat.

Herein lies man's faculty of intuitive leaps and altruistic motivation;
love, service, intuition, spiritual evolution, inspiration for 'excelsior' and higher imagination.

Meditation interlinks "self" and infinite within
and then, one experiences that freedom of one's soul from body-cage even while being within.

Finally, comes the path of unselfish actions
through which, one establishes rapport with all, exhorts greatest influence and enjoys beautiful interactions.
When we're without thought of self, our best work is done.
Since, unselfishness is the other name of God, and all evil forces get humbled without the use of any gun.

All these path-ways lead one to inner peace and bliss.
One realizes then the infinite strength, knowledge and power of "self" within, without a miss.

Divinity and fulfilment is achieved only by one who, works whole heartedly for the good of others.
While, following principles of ethical action expecting fruits

for all and not only for self, as if, for his own brothers.

Essence of "Gita" is deep rest amidst intense action.
When one makes restless mind calm, one can experience spiritual ambrosia like power, joy, contentment, confidence, bliss and inner satisfaction.

Most of management failures are attributed to inadequate attention to means and eye for detail.
That's why, projects with even attainable goals completely fail.

Managers must understand cause and effect relationship in it's totality.
Unless one removes the cause, effect would remain in same form or manifest in duality.

A manager must share his worker's work, genuinely feel for them and be pure in body and mind.
In order to attract them with rare bio-magnetism, which, will compel them to do what managers desire them to do in unbreakable bind.

A manager must remain calm and accept all situation with equanimity.
In success and failure, he shouldn't forgive to show his magnanimity.

In failure, instead of giving up to despair and frustration,
a deep introspection with calmness would reveal where one went wrong and suggest ethically pragmatic means for hope and reverberation.
Management needs to be attempted with visible initiative, enthusiasm vigour and spirit of creation.

Unflinching belief in the fact that every moral value stands on and is nourished by the spirit of self-sacrifice, is, the trigger in otherwise tardy life.

Our forefathers have, thus, by balancing duty consciousness, action, vigour, faith with unselfishness has made it a meaningful and joyful strife.

Fearless Calmness in crisis and quick decision in action are the hall-marks of a good manager
and, in the realm of leadership, there's nothing more infectious than the personal example of a leader.

Religion is the manifestation of natural strength that is in a man.
With faith in self and Him, channelisation of divinity within, with ease, one can.

Excellent leaders are distinguished by the sincerity and pervasiveness of their concern for men.
Both remain inwardly involved in converting their workplace into a zen.

Hindu scriptures have prioritised detached actions over economics, natural principles over profit, absolute quality over quantity, country over religion, man over money and pure values over wealth.
These principles in practice alone, could, ensure our planet's prosperity, richness and superb health.

Leaders with only 'skill-strong" or "value-strong" are going to be misfits in future.
"Skill-strong" and "Value-strong" only have the key to a successful future.

Heroic elements of the west with calm virtues of Hindus
combine would, enshrine all dynamic forces of this world
And, no one can generate enthusiasm and zeal in others
unless, one is not lit with spiritual enlightenment and grace
within one's own world.

With a clean and benevolent heart and mind, managers are
required to realize the strength, opportunities and threats in
store.
and, analyse the practical means to cope up, with spiritual
ethos at it's core.

Future will belong to enterprises which are people driven
and only those, would, deliver results who, are motivation
driven.

Organisations will be required to meet varied tastes and
demands and fast changing preferences of people in
shortest possible time-frame.
Work-force, their 'mind-set', organizations, work-culture
would provide the strategic advantage in a different ball-
game.

There is no doubt that those, who, could cope with
deregulated environment, fast-changing technologies and
market would ensure in future their rightful place.
Innovations will come from only committed and competent
people and which would be a major source of solace.

Technological edge, once achieved, would, erode quickly
and therefore, would need constant review.
Therefore, faith in excellence in work as the highest form of
religion, as a life concept, has the requisite clue.

Technological innovations of today are only human extensions designed to make life more comfortable, convenient and easy.

If the same is misunderstood, it's ill-use would then make the same life more miserable, suffocating and hellishly busy.

Therefore, our audacities in technological innovations must match tenacities of our minds in their use.

and therefore, let the "Synergy" be provided by synchronized explosions of human creativity to make life on our mother planet, a smooth comfortable and enjoyable cruise.

We must understand the adaptable nature of technology as a result of which, human species on the face of earth, still survive.

Towards the goal of paradising our earth, noble and benign management of these technologies alone, could guide.

Materialistic pursuits have fired human imagination and fuelled spirits to innovate and create.

Without sprititual pursuits, such innovations and creations have potential to make humanity suffer and in real terms, degenerate.

Let work not become a mere appendage to machine or a chip

and, let the spirit behind work, not allowed to get out of the spiritual grip !

We have to constantly ask ourselves who is slave; technology or us !

Remember, unless, we, as benevolent human race, don't remain in commanding position, the whole cumulative effort is not even worth a fuss.

Managers for better result, must understand that numerous streams from different directions finally meet in one ocean. Similarly, numerous religions guide their followers in pursuit of one common goal and emotion.

Without which, they would keep wandering in many a form. Experiencing transitory pleasures and pains while going through smooth stretches and bumpy rides amidst ravaging many a storm.

Managers must understand that - followers of different religions lead their lives in different ways.
Remember, source of life is one like the sun and its numerous rays.

It doesn't mean that one is leading life in a better way than the other.
In fact, they must realize that each one is spiritually inter-linked like, the uniovular twin brothers.

"Love thy neighbour" is a concept at micro and macro level worth practice in life by all.
It is then alone, positivity and enrichment in life of all, would snow-ball.

Love fosters love and sharing of other's sufferings also begets love and promotes a healthy bond.
Love then, compels evils like distrust, malice, hatred and greed from ones' life, abscond.

Requirement today, is to understand "self" and His

Creation.

Therefore, it would be easier to fathom His own spark in all living beings and a mind-boggling enchanting range of His manifestation.

This span of life is only means of achieving final goal; realization of oneness, of the whole creation and self as immutable and indistructive part of the great cosmic soul.

In our dogged and fanatic approach to life, we've gone too far.

In the process, our visions are channelled into narrow tunnels where, there isn't a glimmer of hope near or far.
The inherent drive in every human to achieve spiritual growth, is a positive force.
However, display of hatred, selfishness, anger, greed, ego put together, can or leads a person on a negative course.

It is vital to understand that ends and means are both important.
Incompatibility between the two, would otherwise, turn the life-note rather discordant.

Managers must know that, while it is easy to imitate technology, it is important to copy culture.
Affecting this fundamental change in people's mind set would, imbue strategic advantage to any organizational structure.

Working with people, not replacing or down-sizing their activities will be critical for corporate enterprises hereafter.
People then, instead of being termed as just "Cost and Product" would be called "Process and Sources" of power

thereafter.

Corporations with such an ethos and orientation towards their work-force could only adapt to fast-changing environment and manage fierce competition ahead.

Only highly inspired group of people with high aspirations could, innovate, leverage resources, reset boundaries and diversify around core competence and usher in organizational capability and stability instead.

Ethical Culture and work-ethos would enhance flexibility which in turn, would equip people to accept rather than resist change.

Enlightened work-force of an organization would, in external shocks and internal turmoils, keep their cool and not feel estranged.

Critical issue confronting most nations is, today, how to manage change while minimizing cost and enhancing quality.

Answer lies in pursuance of global vision and promotion of ethical management philosophy which, transcends national identity.

Think globally and act locally, think locally and act globally are the by-words.

A change in "mind-set", the way we look at globe, technology, institutions and people are the real key-words.

Strategic advantage in the next century, will go to those, who, would know how to manage people and work-force.
Organisational Culture, Capabilities, values, beliefs and people motivated to deliver performance will, only, set a

successful course.

Innovations will come about only from people with unruffled and unflinching sense of commitment and professional competence.

Sincerity, dedication and devotion could, only, have the way and that too, without any pretence.

People sometimes, have transparent outputs and interests; undiscernable.

Working with people and getting resources through people is also, sometimes not palpable.

We need to reflect whether our work is an "end" in itself or a "means" for creating a workable future !

We, certainly, need to integrate ecology, economy and mother nature and to that end, explore as to how these interact with 'one-n-other'.

Most developing economies of the world with the advent of third millennium are in the throes of a historic metamorphosis,

a mosaic of hither to unknown problems and opportunities, weakness and strengths, despair and hope and a rare chance of glorious historical osmosis.

In this new dawn of world history, ancient wisdom of India is panacea for many a foreseeable challenge and ill.

It, could, help bring about balance between conflicting pulls and pressures and all tensions and worries, most savagely, it would kill.

Since times immemorable, Indians recognized business a legitimate human occupation and businessman as a respected component of society.

Wherein, business community understood their role of creating wealth through righteous means and their responsibilities towards others in it's entirety.

Departmental philanthropy on businessman's part, fetched them social recognition and spiritual merit.

In the ancient cooperative endeavour of Hindus, "Satya; truth, Ahinsa; non-violence and Aparigraha; non-grabbing were most essential facet.

Hindu's philosophy offers a model to help us optimise career cycle for today and tomorrow.

It invites a person to consciously transit through five stages; detailed work, conceptualization, meditation, renunciation and peace in order to be absolutely thorough.

This model, besides enlightened self interests of the individual, offers pure altruistic, ethical injuction
and, thus, provides true empowerment in the organization and facilitates growth as an inherent function.

Indian philosophy has recognized the value of learning, as well as it's limitation.

Also, recognized the distinction between manas (mind) and buddhi (intellect) insight, wisdom and sense of discretion.

While "Buddhi" helps the learner to guide the "Manas" for effective learning in right direction and the philosophy in it's holistic approach to management, supports the view on third dimension (Head, heart and soul).

Indian software tools, Upanisad (sitting close at the knee of Guru for learning), Prasna (Raising questions), Pariprasna (raising counter-question), Yatra (Travel especially, on foot), Tapasya (Penance, concentrated meditation of chosen subject) and Rin (debt) are unique in their nature and concept.

and, also, the lives of ascetics and sages who, devised and practiced such techniques, proved beyond doubt, that, example is better then precept.

Each one of us need to realize that, we, besides our body, mind or Buddhi'; wisdom are linked and are part of a cosmic soul.

It alone, then, would impel each one of us to strive relentlessly for life's selfless goal.

Besides, it's a great feeling to know that all of us are children of Brahma; the creator who is deathless, formless and immortal (Amritarya Putra concept).

It could, thus, energise and invigorate each one of us to do immortal feats even when, our physical self is mortal.

Creation of wealth for society is no doubt the central role of any enterprise and to do so, is, more than wise.

Therefore, in the bargain, it should heal the societal wounds; poverty; illiteracy, disease, natural disasters in it's disguise.

Hindu's (Sangathan Dharma), the corporate responsibility hinges on two cardinal planks;

Ethical means for creation of surplus and distribution of part of it for unliftment of society's lower ranks.

If we see the entire man-kind a one large family (Vasudev Kutumbakam concept), and work under one God's banner (concept of Vasudha).

We, could easily, confront, any kind of 'isms' and integrate global economy in peaceful manner.

We need to realize that heterogenous world of today is, indeed, a rare asset for entire human race.
To begin with, we have with us collective multidirectional and multifaceted wisdom as a common base.

Amidst many worries about the future of our planet and mankind, we need to forge ahead with full faith in our destiny, His providence and grace.
if we succumb to threats like over-populations, desertification, soil erosion, salinity, ozone layer holes, deforestation, nuclear disasters etc. because of our selfish interests, we'd drastically retard our 'march forward' and requisite place.

Blood of the responsible people in responsive organizations pulsates for strides towards forward movement, action and results.
Those, who would allow themselves to be pushed, threatened and controlled from outside in third millennium, would, face ignominy and insults.

The definition of responsiveness is, certainly, in for a change.
Commitment of oneself to goals and targets, to performance and tasks, to action and results shouldn't sound strange.

Commitment and consistency shall have to go hand in hand.

Striving for excellence and peak performance would be the hall mark of any successful band.

Work culture of initiative in which, workers without any inhibitions, could, unfold their talent and skills would be, the order of the day.

Only responsive organizations, which, would grow with their employees and world society together, would, have their say.

Evolution for external management to self-management, self-motivation, self-pride, self-control and self-responsibility are the magic ingredients of individual growth.

Loyalty and total commitment at the time of induction, shall have to be the employee's only oath.

Planning shall have to be based on holistic understanding of man.

Because, tangible result-achievement, only active and proactive individual, rather than a passive element in a faceless system, possibly, can.

Stimulation for a balanced growth and liveliness of people shall have to be the central issue.

Motivated, active and responsive individuals at the grass-root level could only energise an otherwise, dead tissue.

Valuable contribution to an organization comes in a climate that encourages individuals to take risks, put their heart and soul in work, while their spirits gleam.

Express their creative talents, potential and experience a sense of high self-esteem.

This kind of climate, when generated, people share their powers and fears.
True feelings get converted into action, supportive openness and trust in which, they share each other's joy and wipe each other's tears.

Leadership that springs inspiring love, inturn, begets compassion, non-violence and more importantly, a spiritual orientation to both work and life.
Then alone, led get that magnificent feeling of reward and a meaningful strife.

Work place is a place of religion where, heart and soul of each body, comes together to work in union with all others. The environment of mutual respect, trust and feelings of personal well being that, values the softer aspects of our human nature, helps in creating bondage of blood-brothers.

Leadership without truth, is, like a tree with no roots.
It'll stand for a while but, as the winds of challenge and change blow, it'll, in no time, fall to people's boots.

Today, more and more people are demanding the truth and aren't prepared to settle for less.
Therefore, work in most organizations, where people are demanding more truth and management hiding it, is reduced to a mere game of chess.

In the days to come, degree of separation from "roles" to "souls" would dictate percentage achievement of goals
and the absence of the latter, would leave obvious yawning holes.

In the presence of "Truth" alone, conscientious leadership can emerge
and then alone, genuine creativity and communication can surge.

There is need to listen to the inner quiet voice within to unfold the wealth of potentials.
This inner prompting would help one make decision that are high in integrity and help prove in turn, one's bonafides and credentials.

There is, also, a need to redefine, what do we mean by 'sustainable growth', 'economic health' and 'environmental sensitivity'.
Correct comprehension of these then, will need truthful translation into corresponding altered behaviour and activity.

Global development means that, all people lead a full and productive life ;
balanced, harmonious, inter-dependent on each other and deeply involved in a common goal-oriented strife.

It warrants everyone to have, first and foremost, an outward and visible sign of spiritual grace.
A clear conscience and inner depth to see through materialistic mist and haze.

Remember, sound work ethics, ethos and culture sprout from a pristine spiritual base.
Workers, managers and entrepreneurs of such organisations, will always have beaming and fearless face.

A global manager of third millennium, needs to have extraterrestrial vision, dedication, devotion, die-hard professionalism and a fine sense of precision.

These qualities will automatically germinate if, you have faith in self and divine love for His entire creation.

Belief in the ancient Indian concept of matured balance of materialism and spiritualism, would, get one on one single high-way without diversions, side roads and round-abouts, where upon, one could speed up to only destination (success) without tensions, worries and doubts.

Like a silk-worm, let there be no one who, in his own materialistic cocoon, becomes prisoner or a slave and then, morbids this entire precious span from cradle to his grave !

❏

MY SUBMISSION TO THE READERS

Undoubtedly, management is a complex subject
as it deals with both heart and mind
Yet it's an enchantingly limitless field worth
millions of explorations and expeditions, I find.

It implies managing own and other's life.
Management of both pleasures and pains of worldly
strife.

New views of management open up to a fertile,
inquisitive and knowledgeable brain.
A clear grasp on the horizons and under-currents
on the above mentioned subjects would be, I'm sure,
anyone's genuine, in real terms meaningful - gain.

Maturity lies in having knowledge and it's good use
in practice in day to day life.
In order to make meaningful contribution for a
comfortable and totally satisfying whole humanity's
strife.'
My aim and attempt here had been to fuel imagination
and sharpen vision of any knowledge - seeker.
Remember, all secrets and truths lie in a small lab
test tube or a beaker.

With two swords namely knowledge and dedication
in one's hands, a manager can achieve fascinating
goals
and, can perform for the betterment of world society a
variety of roles.

Now you could go all out to face challenges of the new
world with a stout, truthful and honest heart
and sincerely help alter own and other's lot !

❏